# THE
# COLLEGE
# CHAPLAIN

# THE COLLEGE CHAPLAIN

**A Practical Guide to Campus Ministry**

## Stephen L. White

THE
PILGRIM
PRESS
Cleveland

*To my wife and son,*
*partners in ministry*
*and companions of life*

**Andrea Saville White**
*and*
**Aidan Saville White**

*and to my beloved daughter*

**Christen Schubert White Cranford**
*December 10, 1979–November 3, 2002*

The Pilgrim Press
700 Prospect Avenue
Cleveland, Ohio 44115-1100
thepilgrimpress.com

© 2005 by The Pilgrim Press

All rights reserved. Published 2005

Printed in the United States of America on acid-free paper

09  08  07  06  05     5  4  3  2  1

**Library of Congress Cataloging-in-Publication Data**
White, Stephen L., 1949-
    The college chaplain : a practical guide to campus ministry / Stephen L. White.
        p.  cm.
    Includes bibliographical references (p.  ) and index.
    ISBN 0-8298-1677-1 (pbk. : alk. paper)
    1. College chaplain. 2. Church work with students.  I. Title.
BV4376.W45  2005
259'.24 – dc22
                                                                    2005048894

# Contents

——— ✠ ———

1|2|10

# Acknowledgments

——— ✠ ———

**M**Y FIRST-YEAR Latin teacher in high school was never more than a chapter ahead of us in the textbook. He managed to teach us Latin by learning it himself. At the time this struck me as odd, but I have later come to realize that it is sometimes better to teach someone else something that you have just recently learned yourself, while it is still fresh and new for you. Medical students are said to learn to do procedures by "Watching one, doing one, teaching one." As a relatively new chaplain myself I offer you the product of my own "on-the-job training," which, as much as anything else, is based on my making mistakes and trying to learn from them.

Whoever thinks publishing a book is a solitary undertaking never wrote one. I am indebted to many friends and colleagues and to my family for the innumerable ways they have helped me. They have taught me much and have shaped my thinking about how best to be a campus minister and have made numerous contributions to whatever is good and useful about this book. Whether or not named below, each of them has been a blessing and gift from God to Whom I give my praise and thanks.

My friends and bishops, the Right Reverend George E. Councell and the Right Reverend David B. Joslin, have been great supporters of my work at Princeton, as have the members of the Procter Foundation, especially Vice-Provost Katherine T. Rohrer, Jan Logan, Prof. John V. Fleming, the Reverend Leslie Smith, Ev Pinneo, the Reverend Joan Fleming, and Sophie Glovier.

My friends and colleagues at Princeton University have provided me with both a spiritually and intellectually stimulating environment in which to minister. I thank especially Dean Thomas Breidenthal and Dean Paul B. Raushenbush of the Office of Religious Life, Father Tom Mullelly of the Aquinas Institute, and the other members of the United Campus Ministries group at Princeton.

Brother Bede Mudge of Holy Cross Monastery in West Park, New York, and the Rev. Suzanne Guthrie of Cornell University have been invaluable sources of love, support, and guidance during my time at Princeton.

Three wise friends and colleagues read the entire manuscript and offered many comments and suggestions that improved the final product: Dean Thomas Breidenthal at Princeton, the Reverend Greg Bezilla at Rutgers — the State University of New Jersey at New Brunswick, and the Reverend Jennifer Baskerville-Burrows at Syracuse University. Whatever shortcomings remain are, of course, mine.

My friend and colleague Prof. Ellen Charry at Princeton Theological Seminary has helped me sharpen my theological reflections in numerous ways, and I am deeply grateful to her for that and for her encouragement and enthusiasm for this project.

Princeton students from the classes of 2000 to 2008 have been my greatest teachers as I have learned — and continue to learn — how to be a chaplain, often by making — or nearly making — mistakes which they gently and graciously pointed out to me along the way. What a joy and blessing it has been for me to work with the likes of Stanford and Lucy Adams, Uchenna Ukaegbu, Marla Conley, Will Fox, Laura Schutz, Stacia Birdsall, Liz Rockett, Sarah Wood, Rob Simmons, Christopher Wendell, Kristen Bethke, Anne Throdahl, Spencer Compton, Dylan Hogarty, Clare Sully, Owen Hehmeyer, and so many others who have passed through Princeton and have enriched the Christian community here. Students at Princeton Theological Seminary and Westminster Choir College have also been wonderful teachers and supporters of our ministry, especially Hilary Cooke, Susan Richardson, and Kevin O'Malia. Similarly, it has been a blessing to be a friend and pastor to such wonderful faculty and administrators as Prof. Peter Brown, Prof. Elaine Pagels, Prof. Edward Champlin, Prof. John Fleming, Kathy Rohrer, Frank Ordiway, Jan

Logan, Prof. David Billington, and many others. My friend and colleague the Reverend Margaret Hodgkins has also been a great help in so many ways. Each of them has taught me something that has found its way into this book.

I would also like to thank John Sully and Kathy Rohrer, Clare Sully, Joy and Dudley Saville for all their love, encouragement, and care in so many ways.

I wish also to thank my editor, Ulrike Guthrie, for her enthusiasm for this project from its very beginning and for the many ways she has used her extraordinary gifts to make this an immeasurably better book than it would have been if I had been left completely to my own devices.

It is a cliché for clergy to refer to their spouses and families as partners in ministry. But a ministry that is based in the same building where we live has made it inevitable that my wife Andrea and our son Aidan would be drawn into the life of my ministry with students, faculty, and staff. Each in their own way has contributed to the vitality of our common life and ministry and, by extension, to this book. Without them nothing much else would matter, and I joyfully and gratefully dedicate this book to them and to my beloved daughter Christen.

Chaplains of other faith traditions, ages, genders, and with other experiences of life and of ministry, and those writing in a different place or at a different time would have produced a book very different from this one. Perhaps some among them will be challenged to take up their pens to complement the conversation I have begun here. My hope and prayer is that many will find in this book something that will enable them to bring to bear all of their own particular experiences, backgrounds, and gifts of the Spirit for the strengthening and flourishing of campus ministries, which are so vital to the future of both the church and the world.

Introduction

# The Office of Chaplain

*The duties of one who conducts services and provides religious guidance to members of a college or university community.*

———— ✠ ————

I LOVE walking around campus the first weekend in September when the incoming class of freshmen arrives and begins moving into their dormitory rooms. The place is electric with the sense that everything is new and full of possibilities. The anxious looks of parents are in sharp contrast to the smiles and the eagerness of the students who realize that this is their place, not their parents'—and in their place they will find out who they are and become who they will be.

A few days later classes commence and things settle down and begin to get serious—except on weekends, when the most dedicated late-night revelers can be seen wandering home early in the morning when I go out to find the newspaper on the sidewalk. As they settle into the academic year students make choices about what to do about church. Reflecting the secularization of our society, most choose to do nothing. Or perhaps doing nothing is a reaction against parental pressure to go to church. But others begin to search for a way to discover and explore their spiritual dimension. This exploration ranges from staying with the traditions of their childhoods to going as far from them as possible.

While many students have had a good deal of exposure to religion as children and young adults, many others come from families in which the Sunday morning rituals revolved around sleeping late, reading the newspaper, and participating in soccer games. Many parents of the 1960s and 1970s generations had the benevolent but I think misguided idea that religious choices should be left entirely to their children when they were able to make those decisions themselves. Unfortunately, this strategy, while seeming to maximize freedom of choice, has the paradoxical effect of giving children no foundation from which to explore faith and deprives them even of a language and a frame of reference within which to think through their relationship to God. Young people from such families who yearn for the spiritual often cast about aimlessly, making one attempt after another to learn about God, becoming more and more frustrated in the process. Thus, far from expanding choices, the strategy of not exposing children to a religious tradition at all can actually have the opposite effect.

For some students exploring religious options means finding a Bible study group, and these abound on most campuses. Most are sponsored by evangelical Christian groups like Campus Crusade for Christ, but others can be found at various mainline Christian campus ministries as well. But many students who begin their discovery of the spiritual life with the Bible also soon yearn for something more. Bible study groups often have a difficult time being disciplined and staying on task. A group's attempts to study one of the Pauline letters often will devolve into tangential discussions about matters of particular personal interest to group members and have little to do with the book being studied. Also, many students will begin to ask probing questions about inconsistencies in the Bible or about aspects of historical-critical scholarship they may have encountered in class on in their own reading. Why, for example, are there two creation stories in Genesis and why do 2 Kings and 2 Chronicles give such differing accounts of the same historical events? While these questions can enrich a Bible study group, some groups do not welcome such questioning, and those individuals asking the questions end up feeling frustrated and even alienated from the group.

Many students enjoy a weekly worship service. Some like praise worship that is light on theology and high on glorifying God. Others like more traditional services such as those found in Anglican, Roman

Catholic, and Orthodox liturgies. And others like a variety — sometimes a mass, sometimes a Taizé service, sometimes praise, and sometimes a blend of everything. Most campuses have all these forms of worship — and more — for students to sample and explore their sense of who they are in relation to God.

Some students want even more. Some yearn for a deep sense of the presence of God in their everyday lives. They long to know God intimately, and they want the way they live their lives to emanate from that growing knowledge of God. They are yearning for holiness. And as they begin to make progress toward the quest for holiness — although hardly anyone actually uses the terms "holy" or "holiness" to describe themselves — their love and knowledge of God inevitably awakens a sensitivity to others and a caring for others, too. This love of neighbor demands an outlet of service to others in God's name.

A campus ministry must be all these things for students who are on a journey toward God. To be sure, the journey metaphor is a worn and tired one. And yet it conveys the reality that each of us is moving toward God in a way that is unique to each of us and, at the same time, in ways that everyone shares. It conveys that in this life our quest for God will never end. And it suggests that we are not alone, that we are moving along a road crowded with the saints. Some saints have been on the road longer than others. Some have made good progress while others have taken many side roads, rest stops, and detours. Some can walk by themselves, and some need to be carried; some run, others crawl. But whether one is at the head of the crowd or far to the rear, whether one is running or crawling, together we are all moving steadily toward God.

And, of course, campus ministry is not just about students, although that must be its principal focus. An effective campus ministry attends to the spiritual needs of the faculty, administrators, and staff too. It helps to create a community of believers who can support one another.

With this in mind, this book suggests ways of understanding how a campus ministry can help students, as well as faculty and staff, along their journey. Since it is intended to be a handbook or primer for campus ministers, the focus will be on the various roles that are inherent in being a chaplain. Kenneth Underwood's landmark study of campus ministry in America identified four modes of campus ministry: priestly, pastoral, governance, and prophetic.[1] Barbara Brummett approached the field from a slightly different angle and proposed four obvious roles for campus ministers: pastor, priest, rabbi, and prophet.[2] I have built on both these sources and discuss the roles of chaplain as pastor, priest, rabbi, prophet, steward, herald, missionary, and pilgrim in separate chapters. Finally, I examine some of the opportunities and challenges of interfaith cooperative efforts across denominational chaplaincies.

Before we get to that, however, it may be well to acknowledge a certain foundational understanding of what campus ministry is. I write this book as a campus minister and for campus ministers that share a liturgical tradition — however that may be defined within a particular denomination. By this I mean that I assume an emphasis on both word *and* sacrament. I intentionally embrace a certain sensibility that includes an emphasis on the sacraments and on the incarnation. I also implicitly embrace values of tolerance, inclusivity, and questioning. So, in this book campus ministry is understood to be:

. . . **Celebration of Word and Sacrament.** We gather weekly in both formal (churches and chapels) and informal (the chaplain's home, dorms, etc.) settings to hear the word of God proclaimed and to celebrate the supper of the Lord. This is our central act of worship and community, and it is vital to our sense of who we are and to our relationship with God. "Then he took a loaf of bread, and when he had given thanks, he broke it and gave it to them, saying, 'This is my body, which is given for you. Do this in remembrance of me' " (Luke 22:19).

. . . **Hospitality.** A campus ministry needs a place where students can come to "hang out," study, share a meal, gather before going off on retreat or to a special ministry. It needs a place that feels more domestic and homey than a college dormitory. It must have a place where a student — and faculty and staff — can safely let down their guard and be themselves, especially when they are hurting or confused. A campus ministry needs a place where parents can come in times of a child's crisis and alumni can return to remember good old times. It needs a place where in times of turmoil student groups that have been fearful of bigotry have a safe meeting place — a place where all are welcome. It is a place where homesick or otherwise troubled students come over for a little while to study or relax in a quiet, homelike environment — a place where all are welcome. It is about expanding the circle; it is about proclaiming the gospel in word and deed and conveying to everyone that the church is a place where you belong before you believe or "join up." "Let all guests who arrive be received like Christ, for He is going to say, 'I came as a guest and you received me' " (Rule of St. Benedict, chap. 53).

...**Presence.** Campus ministry is about being around, being available, being seen by being present as a symbol of the presence of, and immediate availability of, God in our lives. Chaplains must be part of the life of the campus in ways that are a witness to the love and abiding presence of Christ. By being seen and known around campus a chaplain will be that much more approachable when someone needs help. "Eighty percent of life is just showing up" (Woody Allen).

...**Caring for One Another.** Campus ministry offers counseling through a crisis in faith or in choosing a major or sorority, visiting the sick at the university infirmary or the hospital, being with someone who needs a good cry — or a good laugh, talking things out and through. Campus ministry is students looking out for other students and reaching out to them when they are in need and helping them get professional attention when they are hurting. Campus ministry is about helping a faculty member who fears appearing to be vulnerable in a competitive academic environment get through a family crisis. "By this everyone will know that you are my disciples, if you have love for one another" (John 13:35).

...**Service to Others.** Campus ministry is involving students in delivering food baskets to the poor and tutoring and mentoring runaway kids, visiting nursing home residents, serving meals and talking to rescue workers at Ground Zero in New York, and participating in a Habitat for Humanity project. "And the king will answer them, 'Truly I tell you, just as you did it to one of the least of these who are members of my family, you did it to me' " (Matt. 25:40).

...**Having Fun.** Campus ministry is watching a classic comic movie or enjoying a spirited board game at the chaplain's home during exam week, an annual squirt gun attack on seniors at the end-of-year cookout in May, going to a football game or concert together — especially to support a friend active in the campus ministry; it is being silly together. "Then our mouth was filled with laughter, and our tongue with shouts of joy; then it was said among the nations, 'The LORD has done great things for them' " (Ps. 126:2).

...**Knowing God.** Campus ministry is going on retreat to a monastery, praying together in silence in the chapel, encountering God in one another, figuring out what we believe and why. "I was glad when they said to me, 'Let us go to the house of the LORD!' " (Ps. 122:1).

...**Equipping the Saints.** Campus ministry is allowing students to stretch themselves in leadership positions. It is encouraging young people to strengthen their own faith by sharing it with others through Bible and theology study groups. Campus ministry is making opportunities for students to preach and lead at worship services and getting students involved in local and national church conventions and other activities. It is raising up lay leaders and ordained leaders for the church's future. " ...to equip the saints for the work of ministry, for building up the body of Christ... " (Eph. 4:12).

◆ ◆ ◆

Why is campus ministry so important, especially in these troubled times? Part of the answer is perhaps suggested by what I have already said about what campus ministry is. But I think there is more.

Does anyone doubt that there is some connection between the wholesale abandonment of campus ministries in the late 1960s and the decline both in the number of young people who are involved in the mainline churches and in the number of young people seeking ordination in the years since then? The pool from which the leaders of the church in 2020 will be drawn are in college right now. What are we in the church doing to reach these young people? How are they being trained, spiritually and intellectually, for the roles that await them? All denominations are looking for ways to increase church attendance as we begin the twenty-first century. Is it realistic to expect that the young people of today will be the lay and ordained leaders of tomorrow's church if they are not engaged fully in the life of the church right now?

And in the absence of thriving campus ministries we have another problem, potentially greater than the one just mentioned. As a church we are failing to minister to young people at the very time when they are most able to appropriate for themselves a faith in God that will enrich and sustain them for the rest of their lives, and indeed when they are most acutely seeking a way to complement the intellectual, physical, and emotional changes in their lives with a strong spiritual dimension.

It is my sense that such desires on the part of young people can be more fully met when there are thriving campus ministries with chaplains and sufficient resources to be effective. In my own ministry, I have found the experience of two campus ministries at Princeton University to be instructive.

In 1925 the Episcopal bishop of New Jersey and his wife established a foundation for campus ministry at Princeton University. The first full-time chaplain had been hired a few years before by nearby Trinity Church, whose rector began the ministry in 1867. The bishop and his wife, an heir of the Procter & Gamble fortune, bought a house near campus that is the chaplain's home and a meeting place for students. The foundation pays for the chaplain's salary and benefits and for the maintenance of the house. Procter House has become an important venue for regular worship, fellowship, Bible study, shared meals, relaxing with games or movies, and just "hanging out."

The Presbyterian chaplaincy at Princeton also had a grand old house just a few doors away from Procter House. This house was sold in the 1950s, and the chaplaincy, which is also endowed and has a full-time chaplain, based itself in a large Presbyterian church adjacent to the Princeton campus. Today this campus ministry is staffed by a gifted and energetic full-time chaplain.

Attendance at Presbyterian worship services and other activities is a fraction of that at Episcopal services and activities, largely, I believe, because there is no "homey" center for the Presbyterian campus ministry as there is for the Episcopal ministry.

The situation is worse for many other campus ministries of all denominations. Widespread funding cutbacks gutted campus ministries in the 1970s, and few have fully recovered. While numerous clergy and lay leaders were raised up from the ranks of campus ministries before the 1970s, this has been true in only a few places since then.

The lesson of the Episcopal ministry at Princeton for the future of campus ministries of all denominations is clear. They must have substantial, secure, and independent funding so that they will survive as future budget priorities shift. In order to accomplish this, each denomination must give priority to identifying and securing funds for campus ministry endowments. Typically this will mean that church leaders and campus chaplains will work closely with leaders of local churches to identify potential donors among alumni whom they will approach for large gifts precisely for this critically important ministry. This will inevitably mean that something else will have to have a lower priority.

Many churches engage in campus ministry — formerly called "college work" — funded out of their annual budgets. In some cases these budgets pay for full-time chaplains who have program budgets as well. In other cases, the appearance, if not the fact, of doing campus ministry is maintained by providing a small stipend to priests and ministers who go to the nearby campus to officiate at a sparsely attended weekly worship service. In these cases the chaplains, who have other full-time duties elsewhere, are not able to enter fully into the life of the campus, and they are not able to get to know students, faculty, and staff in a way that might lead to meaningful pastoral relationships. The argument is made that this is "better than nothing," and perhaps it is. But in both cases the lesson of the late 1960s is that national church or parish budgets are subject to shifting priorities, and particular programs — like campus ministry — could be cut at any time. Once a budget line item is cut and the funds are allocated to other programs, it is extremely difficult to get those funds back for their original purpose.

I boldly suggest that any approach to funding campus ministries other than through restricted endowments of sufficient size to fund a full-time chaplain and a meaningful program merely gives lip service to campus ministry and willfully neglects the future vitality of our church. This is not to say that other models will not work and ought not to be pursued. There are plenty of thriving ministries on campuses that have no paid staff and no funding whatever (the Episcopal ministry at Rutgers University in Camden, New Jersey, is a superb example). But it is to propose that stable and secure funding holds the best promise for stable and secure ministries.

In recent years there has been a renewed interest in campus ministry in all the so-called mainline churches that abandoned or reduced this work over thirty years ago. This book is an attempt to share some of the lessons of a particular campus ministry, focusing on the various roles of a chaplain, in the fervent hope that they may be useful in other places, even where circumstances differ greatly. I also hope that this book will encourage others to build up campus ministries where they do not now exist.

If you've seen one campus ministry, you've seen *one* campus ministry! Every campus ministry's strengths and weaknesses are a result of a complicated combination of such factors as the institutional setting and its support or lack of support for campus ministry, the current chaplain's personality and gifts, financial resources, and so on. I recognize that our situation at Princeton is unique in many ways. Ours is a relatively small residential university where the students live, move, and have their being in a bounded space of about two square miles. With few exceptions, all undergraduate students arrive at the same time and graduate with the class they started with four years earlier. We are blessed with a magnificent Gothic Revival chapel — the third-largest university chapel in the world — that is maintained by the university. All of the denominational ministries here are formally recognized by and affiliated with a fully staffed Office of Religious Life. We are supported by a foundation that was established long ago by forward-looking people.

Nonetheless, I believe that much that has been learned at Princeton over the last hundred years can be of use to any campus ministry anywhere. While circumstances differ, the various roles of a chaplain pertain to all chaplains to some degree. I am confident that energetic and creative people throughout the church can adapt many of the ideas in this book and greatly improve on them for their own circumstances. Moreover, the Princeton experience is by no means the last word in campus ministry, and I hope this book will stimulate other publications, seminary courses, conferences, and workshops on campus ministry where "best practices" from other ministries can be presented to the church at large for adoption in other places. I also hope it will encourage national church offices to find ways to offer practical "nuts and bolts" support to emerging and struggling campus ministries at the local levels. I believe there should be a kind of "federalism" in national church offices in which they focus less on programming initiatives and more on identifying "best practices" and infrastructure support for local ministries. Programming is best left to the local level.

We turn now to some of the particular functions of the campus minister — pastor, priest, rabbi, prophet, steward, herald, missionary, and pilgrim. And we will end with a brief look at how all these tasks and functions play out in an ecumenical and interfaith environment.

Some of the tasks will come more easily to some than others will. Indeed, there will be the very human tendency to avoid certain things that seem difficult or that we have convinced ourselves we're "not good at." Thriving campus ministries, however, will be those led by campus ministers who attend to each of these and balance them in their daily work.

# Chapter 1

# The Chaplain as Pastor

*A shepherd of souls;*
*one who protects and guides a group of people.*

——— ✠ ———

**T**HE GREAT nineteenth-century American circus promoter P. T. Barnum is supposed to have said, "You can't sell peanuts unless you get the people into the tent."

The same concept applies to campus ministry. In spite of all our efforts to be visible and to be welcoming, there is always one more person to whom we could get out the word, one more person who doesn't know we're here. I hear the same lament from my brother and sister chaplains in other denominations. The effective chaplain as pastor constantly searches for ways to reach not only those students who may want to "do church," but also those who are alienated from or indifferent to religion. A good chaplain thinks of him or herself as pastor for everyone, not only those who show up for worship services. It's an ongoing dance of gathering in, being present, offering hospitality, caring, and patiently watching young people grow and come into their own.

## Gathering In

Before a chaplain can be a shepherd there must be a flock, and thus the first task for a chaplain is to gather the faithful and the seekers. In parish ministry this is done family by family and person by person, and this is true in campus ministry as well. But in campus ministry a flock is usually gathered class by class. In a residential college the first month or two of term is the season of gathering in the new class and regathering those from previous classes. It is also a time of gathering returning students who may have previously avoided religious services and activities but are now willing to test the waters. In other settings, such as a state university, the gathering process may have to occur more often as the boundaries around a class cohort are not as neatly defined when students matriculate throughout the year. In these cases the gathering may have to occur at the beginning of each new term.

In any case the gathering process is dependent upon the chaplain, student leaders, and the entire campus ministry being visible to new and returning students. On most campuses a bewildering variety of student groups and activities compete for the attention of students. These activities and groups range from sports to drama and dance, from ethnic groups to literary and political societies, along with a wide assortment of religious groups, both denominational and non-denominational. Thus, the chaplain is constantly on the alert for opportunities to make the ministry visible so as to compete effectively in the student activity "marketplace."

"Marketplace" usually has a negative connotation in religious circles, being emblematic of "the world" and all that can take us far from a life in Christ. But our discomfort with thinking of the campus as a marketplace with many secular and religious options — mostly secular, to be sure — can lead us to a passivity and a complacency that will result in a lifeless ministry. Expecting people to come to the occasional worship service, let alone become actively engaged in ministry, just because we think it would be good for them will not work. It takes effort and a commitment to evangelize. Remember — Paul stood in the marketplace and preached. It's where we meet people!

One critical issue is what to call the ministry itself and how to portray the ministry visually. For example, many Episcopal chaplaincies in the United States are called the "Canterbury Club," just as many other campus ministries are called the "Newman Club" or "Aquinas House" (Roman Catholic), "Westminster Foundation"

(Presbyterian), or "Wesley Foundation" (Methodist). Yet it is typically only the *insider* who knows the connection between Canterbury (city, cathedral, archbishop) and the Anglican/Episcopal Church; or that John Henry Newman was a signal Roman Catholic intellectual and convert and Thomas Aquinas is the patron saint of scholars. Because of this, such names tend to work against making a ministry approachable and welcoming. The exception might be those campuses where "Canterbury Clubs" and other like-named denominational ministries are well established and well known. But if a ministry is starting from scratch or reevaluating itself after a period of sluggish activity, a more descriptive name like "The Episcopal Church at..." or "The Methodist Community at..." might be the best choice. After calling itself "the Westminster Foundation" for almost a century, the Presbyterian campus ministry at Princeton recently began to call itself "Princeton Presbyterians," which is much more plainly descriptive. The change has already produced many positive results.

The same can be said for visual symbols of the ministry. Everybody likes to be different and creative. This can lead to campus ministries creating their own emblems and insignia that are really quite idiosyncratic and have no meaning outside the "in group." And with the advent of computer graphics programs that are uncomplicated to use, anyone can design a logo with relative ease. For example, the Episcopal Church at Princeton University developed a logo in the 1980s that superimposed the letters ECP in red over the familiar Episcopal shield. While the Episcopal shield has moderate name-brand recognition, the superimposed acronym obscured the better-known shield and lost any value for attracting people who might have some interest in exploring what was on offer at the Episcopal campus ministry at Princeton. As soon as we dropped the logo with the ECP on it and adopted the more recognizable Episcopal shield, the questions about the meaning of our logo ended. In addition, the adoption of the standard Episcopal logo prompted one of our creative students to devise a graphic that showed the Episcopal shield overshadowing a reclining image of the Princeton University shield, much to the delight of

## The Evolution of a Logo

 The familiar official Episcopal Church shield in red, white, and blue.

 Logo developed in the 1980s for the Episcopal Church at Princeton University (ECP), superimposing the letters ECP on the Episcopal shield. Original shield is obscured, and the "ECP" acronym is not clear. The recognizable church shield is lost, but nothing has been gained.

 Stylized, rounded Episcopal Church shield casting its own shadow that became the basis for a new, more easily recognizable logo.

THE EPISCOPAL CHURCH AT PRINCETON    The new Episcopal Church at Princeton University logo using the stylized Episcopal Church shield in red, white, and blue casting a shadow that is a reclining Princeton University shield in orange and black.

students and alumni who were bemused by the slightly overheated religious overtones of alumni loyalty to their alma mater!

The denominational logos of the Presbyterian Church (USA), the Church of England, the United Methodist Church, the Evangelical Lutheran Church of America, and others are equally recognizable, and this name-brand recognition should be harnessed and exploited rather than replaced. The previously mentioned Princeton Presbyterians make good use of the Presbyterian Church (USA)'s familiar logo by very cleverly substituting Princeton University's orange and black color scheme for the church's red, white, and blue colors.

So-called branding of the ministry is only the first step. The ministry's leadership regularly faces the challenge of identifying students and finding a way to communicate with them. Gathering students into the ministry begins with a list of names, wherever you can find them and however you can develop the list. Indeed, "the list" becomes a near obsession for a chaplain as pastor and student leaders who wish to communicate the activities of the ministry to as many people as possible. And they are constantly vigilant for any opportunity to add a name to the list. By steadfastly focusing on building up the alumni mailing list for the Episcopal Church at Princeton University, the number of names went from under nine hundred names to seventeen hundred in fewer than four years.

Some colleges and universities ask incoming students their religious preference when they register and make this information available, with provisions for confidentiality and data security, to campus ministers. Such lists are maintained by the college registrar's office, and access to the list of students by religious preference is usually through the office of the dean of students or the dean of campus life. Ask around to find out where the list is. Often veteran chaplains from other denominations will be helpful in letting you know where to find information. And do not be discouraged if the list you end up with is quite small. Remember that Presbyterians, American Baptists, and Episcopalians each make up less than 1 percent of the American population, and in some states the percentage is even lower. Indeed, there are more people who believe in UFOs than there are Presbyterians or Episcopalians! But even two or three names can be the start of a core group from which an active ministry can be built, especially when one considers all the unchurched students — some of whom will surely be known to your core group — who may be yearning to develop the spiritual dimension of their lives if they only knew where to begin.

The list, however small, affords the chaplain an opportunity to do several things to make the ministry visible. The first is to make a personalized contact with each new and returning student. One campus ministry at a residential university calls this "the freshman drop"; this package of information includes a booklet geared toward the spiritual journey of college students;[3] a brochure describing the ministry, including times and locations of worship services and other regular events; and a letter of welcome from the chaplain and student leaders. The letter emphasizes the many ways the ministry has played a positive role in the lives of the student signatories to the letter. A small wooden cross key chain that has been very popular is also included. The envelope is then personally delivered to each new student's dorm room by one of the student leaders of the ministry. The list of new students provided by the institution also allows the chaplain to create an e-mail list that can be used each week to announce the week's services and activities. This list is then eventually added to the alumni list, which is used for fund-raising.

At Princeton, we rely on two particular ways of augmenting our list of incoming students. One is by the increasing practice of local ministers and regional church offices (diocese, synod, presbytery, and the like) of collecting names of parishioners who are going off to colleges and then sending them to the appropriate campus ministries around the country. Of course, this can only be successful if the campus ministry has some national visibility such as through advertisements in national church publications or a listing on a national or local church Web site.[4] The other way is to have sign-up sheets for the e-mail list on hand after worship services and at other events, with student leaders standing by to encourage newcomers to sign up.

Once the list is developed and a system is in place for updating and maintaining it, thought can be given to how it is used to strengthen the ministry. The best use of the list is to communicate all upcoming worship services and other activities to the members of the list on a weekly basis. I have found that e-mailing no more frequently than once a week helps assure that the ministry's e-mails will not be deleted before they are read. By trial and error I've also found that varying the subject line, the name of the sender, and the style and format of the e-mail itself increases the likelihood of its being read. And e-mails from fellows students are more likely to be read than messages from chaplains.

Regular e-mails to a large list will inevitably lead to requests from some students to have their names removed from the list. It is the practice of some campus religious groups to bombard students with e-mails and never to remove names from the list even when students repeatedly ask to be removed. I believe that for a church truly to be open, inclusive, and welcoming, the door must swing both ways. If someone asks to be removed from the e-mail list we do so immediately with a brief friendly note saying we are sorry to see them go and reminding them that they are always welcome to our services and may request to have their name added back to the list at any time. We believe this practice honors the idiosyncratic religious journey of each person and leaves open the possibility that our graceful release of the student may eventually result in that person returning to the church family. More to the point, we firmly believe that ignoring a person's request to be dropped from the mailing list can have a negative effect on a person's perception of the church and may actually decrease the likelihood of that person returning to the fold at a later date, perhaps years after graduation from college. Coercion, like guilt, never won any followers for Jesus.

While parish communities tend to be somewhat homogenous in terms of politics, theology (i.e., what constitutes "orthodoxy"), liturgical practices, views about the authority of the Bible, and other ecclesiastical demographics, campus ministries, especially those in institutions that serve a national or international constituency, will tend to have a Christian population with a wide variety of views, attitudes, and opinions about how to "do church." I believe strongly that it is not the task of the campus chaplain to impose his or her views upon students, faculty, and staff with whom he or she disagrees. Rather, I believe it is the chaplain's task to make his or her own views clear, backed up by sound theological reasoning, and to make plenty of space for differing and opposing views. I am reminded of part of an interview of Archbishop Rowan Williams by the *London Telegraph* just before the peace march of February 15, 2003:

Q: So should all good Christians go on the [antiwar] march on Saturday?

A: No. I think all good Christians should ask themselves why they are going or why they are not going, and have a Christian answer to give.

It seems to me that the task of the chaplain is to help everyone, especially students, discover for themselves why they hold the views they hold and to make sure that those views are not only fully examined, but also rooted in the two great commandments of Jesus to love God and to love our neighbor. This can only be done if one views one's mission as gathering in *all* the sheep, not just the likable ones or the ones of like mind. Embracing diversity means, among other things, sincerely celebrating doubt, questioning, making room at the table for unorthodoxy and orthodoxy (whatever that may mean), liberalism and conservatism. Celebrating diversity with real integrity means being in the same church with people who disagree strongly with you and making them feel as warmly and sincerely welcomed as those who are like-minded.

## Being Presence

Another way for the campus ministry to be visible is to have a table set up at one or more prominent locations on campus when new students are moving in. The table could offer a cooler of lemonade and some cookies along with brochures about the ministry. A banner with the ministry's name and the logo of the denomination could be hung from the table's front. If the ministry has enough active students they could help new students and their parents carry boxes and furnishings to the new student's dorm room and give directions to locations on campus.

Holding regularly scheduled and well-publicized office hours is another way to meet students and be visible on campus. But I don't mean office hours in the literal sense of waiting in your office for people to come by. Instead, I mean finding a table at a well-trafficked location on campus such as the student union or campus center. A place near mailboxes and food is the best because it assures a steady stream of passersby who will notice that there is a priest or minister around—especially if you wear your clerical collar, which I strongly recommend. I usually bring a magazine or a book with me to my "office hours" at Princeton's campus center just in case no one stops by for a chat. But I have never finished more than a couple of paragraphs before someone sits down for a visit. Even those who do not stop are vaguely aware of the presence of some "religious character" who seems friendly and approachable enough, and one should not underestimate the long-term value of that kind of "ministry of presence." A small stand-up card on the table with words like "Take a minute to chat with the Lutheran chaplain!" can be all it takes to entice a bashful but interested student to sit down and visit, even just to satisfy his or her curiosity.

Being seen around campus at various events and functions is another way to be present. There are many ways to be seen, such as going to parties, public lectures, and athletic games and events. To be seen regularly "out and about" around campus is a great way to establish oneself as a bona fide member of the community, and thus as someone to turn to in times of crisis.

Being present on campus as a witness to Christ is not something the chaplain as pastor has to do alone. An important way of being present and ministering pastorally to students is through their own peers. There are many models of peer ministry programs in which students work with an ordained chaplain to provide services to the campus. Some are paid and some live in the campus ministry's facility. Others are part of a more informal network of students who are affiliated with the ministry. The Evangelical Lutheran Church of America has taken a lead in this type of ministry, but there are peer ministry programs sponsored by all denominations.[5] Some campus ministries call all their student leaders peer ministers and these students identify, organize, and delegate various tasks and leadership responsibilities to other students in order to maximize student involvement in the ministry at all levels so that everyone's gifts and talents are recognized and used. In other settings the title "peer minister" has a more specialized meaning, often connoting a pastoral role of outreach and caring for other students. In these settings peer ministers, who have closer day-to-day interactions with more students than the chaplain has, are the chaplain's eyes and ears on campus and can help the chaplain intervene in a pastoral situation that he or she may otherwise not know about. Whatever shape a peer ministry program takes on a particular campus, it is a wonderful way to extend the chaplain's ministry and to emphasize the ministry of all baptized people. It is also an excellent way to "equip the saints" for their future ministries in the church following graduation. A chaplain interested in developing a peer ministry program will find many models and ideas on the Internet.

Another aspect of presence relates to how the campus ministry announces itself and makes itself known to the university community. We will have a closer look at this in the chapter on the chaplain as herald.

## Offering Hospitality

During the final interviews for my position at Princeton my wife and I were asked to meet with a group of students. At the time we had recently learned that we were going to have a baby, but we felt it was too early on to tell anyone. During the interview one student asked us if we had a dog. I knew what Amanda was asking. She missed her own dog and her own home and wanted to know whether our home would offer the kind of warmth and domesticity so lacking in a college dormitory. Our answer was, no, we did not have a dog. Months later, however, we joked with Amanda that we had been keeping a temporary secret that we had something even better than a dog — a cute kid! Indeed, our son has, from the beginning, been an important part of our ministry to students just by being around and being himself and therefore providing the sense of family some students are missing.

Recently the new Episcopal chaplain at Rutgers University in New Jersey was confronted with a chaplaincy that had declined, and there were practically no undergraduates involved in the ministry. He spent his first day on the job sitting on the steps of the ministry's house in his clerical collar with his dog lying at his feet. As if for the first time, passersby seemed to notice the house, with its sign saying it is the home of the Episcopal campus ministry.

Procter House has been the principal location and center for the Episcopal Church at Princeton University since 1930. It is a large Victorian house virtually on the Princeton campus, and it houses the chaplain's family and office and has a common room and a basement oratory. Other campus ministries have such facilities such as Aquinas House at Princeton, Brent House at the University of Chicago, the Episcopal Campus Center at the University of Minnesota, and Old Palace, the venerable home of the Roman Catholic ministry at Oxford University. Some campus ministries hold regular meetings and other events at the chaplain's home, although often these homes are not officially a facility of the ministry.

These facilities offer campus ministries a wonderful opportunity to make hospitality a central part of the program. If there is a home involved, the chaplain can offer a guest room to parents who may be in town to be near a student who is hospitalized. We used the guest room at Procter House one semester for a student who had a serious conflict with her roommates until the problem could be resolved.

Even if a home is not a part of the ministry, often a nearby church — as close to the campus as possible (even a few blocks away from the normal "caravan routes" of students may be psychologically too far) can designate a room that can be furnished with comfortable sofas and posters and can serve as a welcoming hangout for students who want a change of scenery. In order for this approach to work, the room must be fully and totally dedicated to the campus ministry and not be used for other purposes. In this way the room can truly become more of a home away from home.

Part of the change of scenery involves food — food that is in any way different and thus more interesting from the standard fare at the dining halls or campus food courts. There's just something about food that brings people together and promotes a spirit of fellowship like nothing else can! Some campus ministries order in food from local restaurants, but this approach misses the opportunity to build community by having students take ownership for menu planning, shopping, cooking, serving, and (this is the tough one) cleanup. At Princeton successful menus and recipes have been computerized so that everything, including detailed shopping lists, can be printed out and so that even the most inexperienced cooks can prepare a first-rate dinner. The Episcopal ministry at the University of North Carolina at Chapel Hill even posted its favorite recipes on its Web site (they're excellent!). Our motto is, "If you can read, you can cook!" Providing snacks during exam times and other high-stress times is also a way to build community and gather in students.

There are some campus ministries that have a small group of bakers who gather each week to make communion bread for the ministry's Eucharists and, while they have the oven hot, a batch of cookies for midweek gatherings and study breaks. Communion bread made fresh each week by the community and offered to God on behalf of the whole community is a powerful symbol of God's abundance and a great way to build up the community itself.

Many parish-based campus ministries have developed "Adopt a Student" programs. Parishioners volunteer to take a student under their wing and invite them on a regular basis to church and home for dinner. This is a great way to make students feel welcome and can be very successful in those settings where the campus ministry has no homey place of its own.

## Communicating Caring

The modern university student does not live by bread alone but by every word that comes by e-mail. Students check e-mail in their dorm rooms and at various public-access computers around campus on their way to and from classes or meals and other activities. Sometimes they check e-mail as a way to procrastinate and other times as a way to use time efficiently. For the college student of today e-mail is as natural a medium for all kinds of communication as face-to-face conversation is and is an important way to be connected to others.

Students often reach out to chaplains through e-mail. Here's a composite sampling of a few I've had (names and identifying information have been altered):

◆ Hey Steve! I was wondering if you and I could meet up sometime to talk. . . . There have been a lot of things going on lately, and I would love to just sit down and talk them out with someone. . . . My schedule is very flexible, so just let me know! Thank you! Jane

◆ I spoke to you last evening about uniting with the church, and I would like to know more about the process involved. I grew up in another denomination, and was confirmed around age twelve. I have increasingly been unable to agree with many of the teachings, and have consequently left. It seems to me that this church is more of a home for me, at least from what I have been able to gather from attending services at various congregations intermittently over the past four years. I would like to be able to discuss this more at length with you sometime. Thanks. Sam

◆ I am having some problems at the moment that I am trying to deal with, and I would like to have somewhere quiet to think about things, maybe sometime tomorrow. Is there any way I could use the small chapel in the basement of Procter House, and maybe talk with you a little? (Again, sometime tomorrow if possible.) Thank you, Charles

◆ I am from China and was raised in a Buddhist home. I am very interested in learning more about Christianity and wonder if you have any time to meet with me. Lucy

These are only the e-mails asking for an appointment. As often as not students will write long, detailed messages expressing frustration, confusion, or anguish, or will pose very specific questions about church doctrine and beliefs or about moral dilemmas. These invite thoughtful responses by e-mail or perhaps an invitation to meet privately in the office or at a coffee shop.

E-mails also offer many opportunities to reach out to students in various ways. For example, after a new student has come to a worship service or other activity, either alone or with a friend, I make a point of sending a friendly message thanking them for coming, telling them about other activities, directing them to our Web site, and offering to get together for a chat. A friendly e-mail to a student who has not shown up at worship or other activities for a long while, or to a student who may be having some difficulty, is a gentle way of letting the student know without pressuring them that he or she has been missed. Also, there are many students who travel at the periphery of the campus ministry, showing up only infrequently for worship or dropping by at the chaplain's office hours occasionally. Yet even such infrequent contacts signal an interest in being connected even when the students are not able to commit themselves to more involvement. An occasional e-mail message from the chaplain inquiring about how they are getting along is an excellent way for the chaplain to show concern without scaring them off.

Another aspect of caring is pastoral care, which takes a variety of forms — many of which are discussed throughout this book. Hospital and infirmary visits are a critical element of pastoral care often overlooked by campus ministers. The role of the parish priest in England offers a helpful model: since the Church of England is the church established by the state, the parish priest views everyone within his or her parish or geographical area, whether Anglican or not, as a member of the parish and will always be ready to reach out pastorally to anyone living within the parish's boundaries. Thus, whenever I hear of a student who has been hospitalized, I drop by to say hello. Likewise, whenever I hear that a professor's spouse or partner is suffering from a severe illness, I mail a card expressing concern and promising prayer, regardless of whether I know him or her personally or whether he or she is Episcopalian or in any way religious. I know my colleagues in other denominations do the same.

Communicating caring requires that the chaplain as pastor maintain strict confidentiality in all interactions with students, faculty, and staff. Maintaining confidentiality is, of course, something that all ordained clergy must be careful about, and a good chaplain knows that a reputation for breaking confidentiality will ruin his or her ability to be a pastor. But campus ministry poses additional challenges. One common one is the concerned parent who wishes to know whether a son or daughter has become involved in the campus ministry and is attending church. I always make it clear to parents and students alike that I will never reveal to a parent whether or not a student attends services or other activities we sponsor. And I say why. To do so would be a violation of the student's privacy and would interfere with the student's process of appropriating the faith independently of his or her parents.

Another challenge with regard to confidentiality has to do with information a chaplain may have about a potentially life-threatening situation. Occasionally a chaplain becomes aware that a student may be having suicidal thoughts. Such students must be referred to competent trained mental health professionals so they can get the help that is beyond the training and experience of most chaplains. The chaplain will play a major role in making the referral and encouraging the student to keep the appointment. The problem arises when the student does not go for help. Does the chaplain have a duty to break confidentiality? This question is made more complicated if the chaplain is employed by the college or university that has a strict policy against reporting anything to the student's parents without the student's permission. I believe that in these cases the wise chaplain will confer with mental health professionals to determine if the threat is serious. If it is, then I believe that it is proper for the chaplain to sound the alarm with university officials — the dean of students, the director of the student health service, and even the campus police. Such breaches of confidentiality are never taken lightly or done without consultation with others who can help the chaplain make the best assessment possible of the risks of maintaining confidentiality. But it is sometimes the highest form of caring to bring a student's potentially life-threatening thoughts and behavior to the attention of those who can help the student, even if the student objects.

Finally, another form of communicating caring is to reach out, and be available to students, faculty, and staff who may be marginalized in some way. Is there a blind student who cannot find her way to the chapel without help? Is there a transgendered faculty member who is isolated from her peers? Is there a group of students who have been persecuted because of their race or skin color? These are just a few examples of opportunities for the chaplain as pastor to be a powerful witness for Christ on the campus by showing concern and care for those on the edges.

One college chaplain recently recounted the highest compliment of her ministry; a student who had come to her to discuss difficulties in relating to her parents said, "I don't censor anything when I talk with you." Fostering a reputation as a caring, concerned, nonanxious, nonjudging, and completely trustworthy pastor is as important a task as there is for a campus minister.

## Watching Them Change

"Come, go down to the potter's house, and there I will let you hear my words" (Jer. 18:2). Before I went to seminary I was in business for many years. In business one often spends many months courting a new customer, trying to win a major contract, or developing a new product or service and then ending up with no results to show for all the effort expended. I can think of numerous examples of customers who chose a competitor, of contracts lost, and of new products that flopped after months of development. Maximum input; minimal results.

In ministry I find the opposite to be true. A seemingly insignificant word or gesture often has a major impact on a person's life. This is particularly true with regard to watching students with whom I have worked develop over their four years at Princeton.

The analogy of a clay pot made by a master potter comes to mind. While it is being made you can imagine from its design and shape how beautiful it will become, but you can *only* imagine. You can't see it in *all* its beauty before it is fired. When the glaze is painted on it doesn't look like much of anything, just shades of earth tones, and nothing like the colors they will be after the pot is fired. Then the potter puts it in the kiln and has to be patient while it is fired for a long time. He has to be patient, and he has to live with the possibility that there might be some air bubble or a bit of moisture in the clay — perhaps in one that has become very dear to him — that will cause the pot to crack and break in the high heat of the kiln. But that doesn't happen very often. Usually, when the pot is finished in the kiln, it comes out hardened and strengthened and with its original shape now adorned with brilliant colors — all of which would have been impossible without the peril of the terrible heat and the anxiety of the potter who waited for this wonderful moment. Now the pot can be put to good use and enjoyed for many years by all who see it. And the potter can smile about what has been created from earth and fire and the endurance of some temporary anxiety.

College students are like pots in this respect. They have to go through fire in order to be strong and to grow and to show all their latent beauty. They have to be able to test all their beliefs and assumptions about everything so that their identities are truly their own and not a reflection of their parents' hopes, fears, and aspirations for them. Thus, the chaplain plays a critical role as mentor and sounding board. In order to help students through the fire that leads to a solid identity the chaplain's caring must be in the form of listening and communicating a regard for each student rooted in a recognition that each one of them is a child of God and of irreplaceable value. And it involves continually asking simple questions like "What would make *you* happy?" or "I know what your parents would like you to do, but what about *you?*" or "Where is God in all of this?" or "What decision would be the best expression of your faithfulness to God?"

It is often difficult for genuinely caring and loving parents to convey this message to their own children without the confounding element of vicariousness or implicit expectations about "good" choices or "right" choices. To use a common example, it is far easier for a chaplain to be totally accepting of a student at an Ivy League or Oxbridge college who yearns to be a teacher than it would be for a parent who may long have harbored dreams of medical school, law school, or a career in investment banking for their overachieving child. As students make decisions about courses of study and majors and jobs or graduate school after graduation, there is often a parallel set of issues related to the student becoming independent from parental influence. This developmental task begins in earnest in college but is rarely resolved completely before a person is into his or her early thirties. Thus, the chaplain will usually not see how things turn out and can only hope to help a student — and sometimes the parents — to set a healthy trajectory toward independence.

The longer a chaplain stays on the job, the harder it may be to endure the yearly cycle of becoming close to certain students in particular and to whole classes in general who, at the end of their time in college, simply vanish one day. A good deal of emotional energy is expended in getting close to students, and as one is a companion to them through four or more years of growth into independent adulthood and all that goes with that growth, over the course of the four years it becomes increasingly difficult to sever those ties, especially when the severing, marked with the high drama and jubilation of commencement, is so sudden. At the end of my first year as chaplain I walked around in a daze for about a week following commencement when the campus, which had been teeming with parents, friends, alumni, and smiling seniors just a few days before, now resembled nothing so much as a ghost town. It was my wife who pointed out to me why I was so glum, and the next year I was a bit better prepared for the exodus of dear students from our lives.

This annual transition has obvious implications for the chaplain's self-care, which I will take up in another chapter. But it also has implications for how the chaplain focuses the direction of his or her ministry. The primary purpose of campus ministry is to serve a *student* population, and a secondary purpose is to serve faculty and staff. Since faculty and staff are a more permanent population, there is a tendency over time for a chaplain who has been emotionally bruised by a long series of good-byes to shift his or her attention away from the transient undergraduate population to the faculty and staff. This is a common phenomenon in chaplaincies with long tenures, and it may be a sign for the chaplain and his or her board of directors that a change is overdue. This self-protective tendency can be warded off by being a part of a colleague or peer group, by having a close friend who loves you enough to tell you things about yourself you would rather not hear, and by having regular spiritual direction yourself.

The task of the chaplain as pastor, then, is to gather students in, to be present to the college community, to render hospitality, and to be a caring person who encourages healthy growth and independence in a spiritual context. We turn now to another aspect of campus ministry relating to the centrality of worship to the Christian community and the role of chaplain as priest. To borrow P. T. Barnum's aphorism, now that we've got the people into the tent, it's on to the peanuts!

## Chapter 2

# The Chaplain as Priest

*One having the authority to administer sacraments
and pronounce absolution; one who presides at
the Eucharist and other worship services.*

——— ✠ ———

W HEN I HEARD that Melissa, a bright, popular sophomore, had been found dead in her dormitory room a few days after arriving back on campus for the start of the school year, all I could think to do was to go to her residential college and be around in case anyone needed anything I might be able to offer. In times like these, there is no thought of an agenda or of exactly what you'll do. It just seems that being around is enough, to offer support and comfort any way you can.

I spoke with quite a few students and staff who knew Melissa, and we said to one another those things that needed to be said. But there was more. One young man I had seen huddled in prayer with other students and who later was pacing about the college approached me and said, "Will you pray with me?" So I put my hand on his shoulder and prayed for Melissa, for her family, and for her friends who were so shocked by her death. I asked God to help us know what to say and do in the days ahead so that we could be a comforting presence to others. When I finished the young man said, "Thank you. That was so helpful!"

A few days later I ran into this young man again, and we spoke about how he and his friends were doing and how very hard it was for all of them to take in the enormity of Melissa's death. He thanked me again for praying with him. So I asked him why it had been important to him for me to pray with him in view of the fact that he had been praying with his friends a few moments earlier. He shrugged and said, "I guess I just needed a minister to say something too."

Shortly after this encounter I met up with a leader of one of the nondenominational groups on campus who had also been at Melissa's college when I was there, and when we compared our experiences he told me that a couple of students had likewise asked him to pray with them. I told him how the young man I had prayed with had said to me, "I guess I just needed a minister to say something too." He shook his head in amazement and said, "That's what the students also said to me! They said they just wanted a minister to pray with them too."

The most important word in this story is "too." These students had been willing and able to pray themselves. But they also wanted a minister to pray with them, someone whom they perceived to have a special role or authority in leading prayers that would not in any way supplant their own prayers, but whose prayers with them and for them would augment their own. It seems to me that this is what the chaplain's priestly role is all about. It is not peculiar to those traditions like my own that call their ordained ministers priests, and it does not suggest that the chaplain as priest prays as a stand-in for those who are not ordained. It is a critically important role that effective chaplains consciously employ to bring those in their care closer to God in prayer; we must be aware of what we do and do not represent.

Kenneth Mason, discussing George Herbert's amazing poem on priesthood titled "Aaron," after the great high priest of Exodus, has this to say:

> The picture of Aaron standing robed before the people of God acts as a ruling conceit organizing all the material of the poem, shaping the poet's exposition of his own experience of priesthood. With that image goes one unavoidable affirmation, that priesthood is a social institution, a form through which people are related to one another as well as to God.... The climax

of the poem is not merely "Aaron's drest" [i.e., dressed], but "Come people, Aaron's drest. . . . " The priest's calling is to represent . . . those things which are considered most vital . . . those truths which are saving truths because they are sacred and sacred because they are saving.[6]

The priestly functions of celebrating the holy communion, blessing, and pronouncing absolution and other sacramental functions take place in the context of a community of faith and are meant, as much as anything else, to enhance and build up that community. The dressed — or vested — priest, far from being an intermediary between God and others, rather leads the people to God, shows the way for others. This connection with God's people is the *sine qua non* of priesthood; without a recognition of this dimension of priesthood, one's priesthood is certainly diminished and may even be altogether annulled. What I will have to say in this chapter may be slightly more applicable to those traditions that use more liturgical styles of worship and that emphasize word and sacrament, rather than only word. It will also emphasize a theology of sacrament that is open to all baptized persons and not restricted to those of a particular denomination. But I believe the connection between the community and the chaplain as priest applies to all in some ways, and I hope that the reader who may not be able to accept every individual tree in this chapter will at least be able to appreciate the overall forest.

In the previous chapter we discussed the various ways a campus ministry gathers people into a community. The principal way that people are drawn to a faith community on a campus is through worship. Even a moderately sized college campus is usually a smorgasbord of Christian worship options, ranging from evangelistic nondenominational praise services to Roman Catholic masses and the Orthodox Divine Liturgy.

Services of the holy communion at which the table is open to all baptized Christians (or, indeed, to everyone, whether baptized or not) represent a unique option on a college campus, just as they do in the community at large. Whereas the evangelical praise services serve to emphasize the immediacy of Jesus Christ as Lord and Savior, and Roman Catholic and, especially, Orthodox worship — as well as most forms of Anglican worship — tend to emphasize more of the numinous and the transcendent, open liturgical worship, at its best, can be a powerful vehicle by which God as friend and brother in the person of Jesus Christ *and* God as wholly (and holy) other can be praised and worshiped. The common meal of the communion offers a dimension to worship available to all that, for many, complements the praise worship of evangelical services and provides a glimpse of the holy that is unavailable elsewhere. In addition, the centrality of the Eucharist and its openness strengthens the sense of community and *koinonia*. This then becomes the central function of chaplain as priest — to preside at the welcoming yet transcendent and transforming gathering of Christians and seekers who wish to know God in the breaking of the bread.

## Regular Worship

The chaplain's main public function is the leading of regular worship. At a residential university like Princeton, the main worship service of the week can be held on Sunday. At universities where a large percentage of the population leaves the campus on weekends, a weekday or evening is a better choice. In any case, a day and a time that suits student schedules is essential, which calls for some flexibility on the part of chaplains as well as faculty and staff. For example, even though the Princeton weekly Episcopal Eucharist is held on Sunday, it is at nine o'clock at night — not a time that is convenient for faculty and staff, but a perfect time for undergraduates for whom, I am told, this hour is roughly equivalent to my noontime. The target population — rightly undergraduate students for most campus ministries — should be consulted about the best combination of day and time for weekly services. And you will want to revisit this question every year or two in order to be sensitive to shifting preferences.

It may make sense on some campuses to hold more than one service per week for different constituents. For example, at Princeton in addition to the Sunday night service, we have an informal house Eucharist at the chaplain's home each Wednesday at 5:30 p.m. followed by a student home-cooked dinner and a guest speaker or, during exam times, games or a movie. We also offer a weekly Eucharist at the local Presbyterian seminary and in the University Chapel. At the University of Alabama at Birmingham, there are several Episcopal Eucharists throughout the week at various outlying campuses of UAB and neighboring colleges. After a period of trying different times, the chaplain and his student leaders there found the most convenient combination of time and place.

## Taizé or Not Taizé — That Is the Question!

As to the kind of regular service on offer, I would argue for a prayer book–based liturgy with a fair degree of predictability and a high degree of reverence. The niche that the Episcopal and Lutheran churches — to cite just two examples — occupy on most campuses argues for an open and welcoming liturgy that is "by the book"; for there are ample opportunities on most campuses for students to experience praise worship and other forms of informal communal prayer. The same might also be said for Methodist, Presbyterian, and other denominational forms of structured worship.

When I was working on a graduate degree at Brandeis University I took a course in economic statistics in the winter term that began at eight o'clock on Monday mornings. Sometimes the heat had been turned off all weekend and the room was unbearably cold when we arrived, and at other times the heat had been left on high all weekend and the room was stiflingly hot. After a few weeks of experiencing the extremes of heat and cold in the same classroom, our professor, an economist with a mathematical turn of mind and wry wit, said, "You know, on the average, it's just right in here."

I often think of this in terms of worship. We sometimes have a tendency to go to extremes in our effort to get it just right. Sometimes we try liturgies that are totally unfamiliar in their shape and content in an attempt to "shake things up" and be relevant to those for whom traditional worship is dry as dust. At other times we embrace the tried and true, the traditional forms of our worship traditions. Whatever extreme we go to will make some feel, in a manner of speaking, too hot or too cold. Maybe on average, as my professor suggested, that's just right. But, then again, maybe not.

Campus ministries are forever seeking the best liturgical approaches for regular worship. Alternative Eucharistic prayers, supplemental liturgies — both from the national church and "home brewed" — and creative adaptations of what is commonly called Rite Three (*Book of Common Prayer*, 1979, pages 400–409) are used widely in Episcopal campus ministries. Similar adaptations of approved forms of worship within a familiar form or "shape" of worship are common in all denominations in America and other countries. Various combinations of Eucharistic worship and periods of silent meditation and songs from Taizé are also popular.[7] There are probably as many opinions about how best to worship as there are ordained clergy (correction: square that number, and you'll be closer to the truth!), and I here offer my own suggestions for worship in a campus ministry context with a great deal of trepidation.

I am reminded of what my eighth-grade English teacher advised in terms of writing an essay: know your audience. Knowing what the majority of the regular attendees like and don't like in the way of weekly worship is something always to keep in mind and, of course, with a student population that is constantly turning over, that is a moving target and a difficult one to hit with any consistency. That is why I am suggesting a preference for a mode of regular worship that is creative and innovative but generally "by the book" — the book in question being the principal approved service book of one's denomination.[8]

There are several good reasons for generally sticking to the denominationally approved service books. One is that doing so will provide a recognizable shape and form to the worship for students from many different places. This is especially important in the case of an institution that draws students from all over the country and even the world. Approved forms of prayer have traditionally been the "glue" that holds the church together, and they can serve the purpose of building up and strengthening a sense of community in a dramatic way on a college campus.

Another reason for sticking to one's denominational worship or prayer book relates to the aforementioned niche of the liturgical churches on the campus. Those students attracted to liturgical worship from evangelical circles will appreciate the stately language and the order and predictability of the prayer book services. One Princeton student who had been attending praise worship services since middle school told me, "My life is so hectic and chaotic, the last thing I want when I worship on Sunday is more chaos. The prayer book is wonderfully predictable, and that is a great comfort to me." He went on to talk not only about the predictable form of the worship, but also its rhythm and what he called the "variety within structure" of the changes in the liturgical seasons. On the other end of the spectrum, students drawn to Episcopal, Presbyterian, or Methodist worship from the liturgical churches because of the open communion policy of these churches will be comforted by the similarities between their communion services and, say, the Roman Catholic mass. These attractive characteristics of worship can be lost if there is too much deviation from approved forms. Those aspects of worship peculiar to other denominations are similarly worth preserving for the same reasons.

The decline in prayer book literacy is another reason to insist on using the prayer book. There once was a time when every Episcopalian brought their prayer books to church with them and could remember the creeds, canticles, confessions, and thanksgivings with ease. One still sees this in a few places, particularly in the American South, but it is becoming more and more the norm for entering college students to be quite unfamiliar with their tradition's service book. This is a terrible loss for the whole church and for each denomination, and I believe that campus ministries can play a role in preserving the prayer book heritage of the various liturgical churches by making it the cornerstone of regular worship.

The regular use of the familiar service books also addresses a pastoral concern, namely, homesickness. If worship at school has a form and content that is recognizably Anglican, or Methodist, or Presbyterian, or Lutheran, etc., and thus familiar, then students from far and wide are much more likely to feel "at home" at common worship. Often I have had students from faraway places like Australia and New Zealand say something like, "Your prayer book is a little different from ours, but not that much. Coming here makes me feel like I'm home." And I recently heard a Presbyterian from California say how good it made her feel to hear a psalm prayer from the *Book of Common Worship* recited in New Jersey.

Yet this preference for the standard service books begs the question of how best to reach young people who enjoy popular music and are more comfortable with expressions of the popular culture than they are with forms of worship that they may associate with the church to which their parents used to drag them on a Sunday morning. Isn't there room for any variation and experimentation? Of course there is, especially in those places where there may not be any other services that offer praise music or other forms of contemporary worship. If that is the case, then a particular campus ministry might well be a place where a wide variety of worship forms can be tried and experienced. It's a case of knowing your audience!

The Episcopal experience at Princeton suggests a number of answers to this dilemma. One is that, since there are indeed many forms of contemporary worship on offer at Princeton, the Episcopal services that are the best attended and the most popular tend to be those that stick to the standard prayer book and hymnal. Nonetheless, there is always demand for a Taizé service, which we hold every few weeks. Some students who always come to the Taizé service never come to any other service, and likewise there are students who regularly attend our Sunday services *except* when we hold a Taizé service. Both types of services are held in the beautiful Gothic Revival University Chapel in the chancel area. But whereas the regular Eucharistic services are somewhat traditional and formal with worshipers sitting in the choir pews, the Taizé service employs the pavement between the choir pews where worshipers sit on the floor on carpet samples with a votive candle near each person and the chapel lights turned down. For Taizé services we set up a small table in the chancel instead of using the high altar, and the celebrant vests only in an alb and stole, omitting other vestments. (See Appendix 1 for an order of a Taizé service that can be adapted to any denomination's form for the Lord's Supper.)

Even when we follow more traditional forms of Eucharistic worship we tend to vary the Eucharistic prayers, using forms not only from the American prayer book, but also, with our bishop's permission, from other members of the Anglican Communion. For example, the five Eucharistic prayers from the Scottish Episcopal Church have a very contemporary feel while maintaining a traditional shape. As Princeton draws students from all over the Anglican Communion, we use Eucharistic prayers from those churches in the Communion from which we have a significant number of students. This always gladdens the hearts of homesick Australians, Canadians, Britons, South Africans, and others who happen upon an Anglican service using prayers from back home!

Eucharistic prayers and forms for the intercessory prayers (i.e., Prayers of the People, Prayers of the Faithful) might also be varied throughout the year according to season, feast, or special occasion. A sign of a vibrant campus ministry with healthy student involvement is a steadily building crescendo of complaints when the worship tends to fall into a rut of any kind. The complaints can be avoided to some degree if students are involved in planning each week's worship. Involving one or more students in weekly worship planning — selecting hymns, Eucharistic prayers, Prayers of the People, and so on — has not only the advantage of assuring that worship is sensitive and responsive to shifting student tastes and liturgical sensibilities that may elude the chaplain, but also offers students who may be discerning a call to ordained ministry a glimpse into the daily work of a priest and gives the chaplain an opportunity to be such a student's mentor. Of course it's also more fun to plan liturgy with a bright, interested student or two than it is to do it alone! In addition to weekly worship planning meetings, the ministry might also consider semiannual reviews of worship forms and practices that involve as many students as possible in a lively debate about how to get worship "just right."

There are many other issues in worship about which there is controversy, such as the use of incense for Episcopalians and how often to have communion for Methodists. Practices vary widely in parish churches, and students come to college with a range of views on such issues. The use of incense in worship and the frequency of communion have many biblical warrants and a rich tradition in Christian worship. Nonetheless, there are many who feel incense can be overused or communion too frequent — or infrequent — and this can be a distraction to worship. It is probably advisable for chaplaincies to find a middle way with regard to these controversies. For example, rather than using incense every week, perhaps using it only occasionally on special Sundays and holy days like Christmas, Easter, and Pentecost would be acceptable to most. Also, during festive seasons like Epiphany and Easter, incense could be used in creative, less dramatic ways so as to have the desired effect of enhancing worship for everyone without distracting from it.

## Political Correctness or Theological Correctness — Take Your Pick!

I used to think I was pretty liberal about everything. Politically, I am pretty much left of center. I care deeply about social justice issues, and in this category I include matters of racial, gender, and sexual orientation justice and equality. I would never want to imply that God is male (or female) or that any aspect of our relationship with God is reserved for some and not available to everyone.

I also believe that it is an important function of a college chaplain as priest to convey this sense that God, through Jesus Christ, is not only available to everyone with no intermediary, but has a preferential disposition toward those who are marginalized or disenfranchised in any way.

Where I tend to find myself thinking more traditionally is when in public worship a priest, to cite just one example, addresses a gender equality issue using questionable theology. For instance, the so-called Father language in the Trinitarian formula "Father, Son, and Holy Spirit" is without doubt problematic from a gender equality point of view, implying as it does to some that God is male. From a pastoral point of view this can be a problem for some women (as well as men) who were abused by their fathers or otherwise experienced unhappy relationships with father figures in their early years, or who feel marginalized in a patriarchic society (and church!).

One solution to this problem often employed is the following quasi-Trinitarian formula: "Creator, Redeemer, Sanctifier." This formula eliminates all gender references and solves the "political" problem, if I may crudely refer to it that way. However, it also unintentionally creates a theological problem or, more accurately, a Christological problem by denying, suppressing, or at least obscuring, the maleness of Jesus. If we want to stress the doctrine of the incarnation, and all that means to us, then we cannot at the same time obscure the humanity of Jesus Christ by making him neuter. Equally, if we wish to remain faithful to the doctrine of the Trinity, we cannot suggest that the functions of creation, redemption, and sanctification are the exclusive role or province of any *one* member or person of the Trinity rather than aspects of the one undivided God, and thus, *all* persons of the Trinity. To do so is to solve a serious gender-political problem by introducing a theological error into regular worship. As to the pastoral problem of unhappy experiences with fathers, emphasizing the fatherhood of God, far from being unhelpful, may be the best medicine of all in a world where a model of ideal fatherhood is desperately needed.[9] Another approach might be to hold conversations in which students can be encouraged to imagine God as mother and to examine scriptural references to God that emphasize qualities that our culture considers more feminine than masculine.

This book is not intended to be a theological treatise, and I do not want to get too deeply into the arguments concerning the theology of gender-inclusive language. However, whenever it does no violence to basic underlying Christian doctrines or to actual scriptural texts, such language should be used; when it does cause such violence, gender-inclusive language should not be used, even when to do so may rectify an implied gender inequality. The reason I want to insist on this is that campus ministries should always be a model of clear and crisp theological thinking. This is critical from a pedagogical point of view as well as one of theological orthodoxy and clarity.[10] I will have much to say relating to this issue in other chapters about the rabbinic and prophetic roles of the chaplain.

Of course it is important to conduct worship in a way that assures that everyone present feels fully and unequivocally included in the deepest and most profound sense not only in the worship itself, but also in every aspect of God's gracious economy. But it is also important that worship services offered for the future leaders of our church convey sound and solid theology and biblical exposition that is as faithful to the original languages as possible. Whenever these two considerations seem to be at odds, I would boldly suggest that orthodox theology and faithful Bible translations trump anything else. Pastoral concerns and confusion about meanings that result from this conflict can and must be taken up elsewhere in the life of the church. It is here, perhaps, where the role of chaplain as priest becomes most clear, because these issues require a kind of leadership that is best designated through ordination rather than expecting the leadership to emerge from the congregation.

Now you know why I *used* to think I was a liberal!

## Celebrating God and Not Yourself

The chaplain as priest, then, is a particular kind of leader with regard to worship. And when there are designated leaders there is a potential for another problem. Henri Nouwen wrote that "The Christian minister is the one whose vocation is to make it possible ... [for others] ... not only to face his [or her] human situation but also to celebrate it in all its awesome reality."[11] It seems to me that this vocation to celebrate the human situation with honesty and integrity calls for a certain humble reverence in the face of God's unconditional and unimaginable love for us. It also seems to me that such a stance of humble reverence can be experienced as truly joyful not only by the celebrant, but also by the entire congregation.

I raise this issue because there is a tendency in ministering to young people to mirror the popular culture in terms of music, discourse, and mannerisms. For example, there are any number of chaplains who are talented musicians whose repertoire ranges from praise music to folk and rock. Integrating these musical styles into worship can be very beneficial. But a problem arises when the priest becomes more of a performer than a celebrant.

In his magnificent short book on liturgical style Aidan Kavanagh counsels against a liturgical celebrant affecting a "loose informality." He writes:

> Breezy liturgical style is not characteristic of one who has attained liturgical mastery. It is usually the work of an egocentric who imagines that whatever occurs to him or her is generally interesting and that uninhibited liturgical expression of this will create enthusiasm and carry the day. It may also be a compensation mechanism of the guilt-ridden or unsure who cannot cope with the fact that some of God's ways are inscrutable and often illiberal according to human standards.[12]

Strong brew, this, but important to attend to. I don't know whether college students are any more able to spot an egocentric than anyone else is; probably not. But I would like to suggest that an egocentric officiating at worship is likely to have a seriously negative effect on a young person whose previous experiences with religion have been unpleasant either owing to parental pressure to participate or his or her own doubts and questions, or both. Such a liturgical style might be the last straw. On one campus in the American Northeast, returning alumni still joke derisively about "Father Hotdog," a former chaplain who famously improvised at the altar and interjected his own ego into sermons and liturgies with maddening regularity.

Not that there is no room for certain types of prayers and worship that do, in fact, purposely adopt a relaxed style. Such forms will, to be sure, be attractive to many, and when prayed publicly from the heart can be powerful and effective. But the main worship services of the week should be marked by the numinous, the deliberate, the reverent. I insist on this not only in the interest of a "decent and orderly" worship — something prized by many traditions — but also to preserve and maintain the priestly role of the chaplain vis-à-vis the undergraduate population he or she serves. While being easily approachable is critically important, a chaplain is mistaken in thinking that students prefer a chaplain to be their friend rather than their priest. Thomas Aquinas asserted that Christ is the source of all priesthood, and thus what is most important is not being "cool" but being "holy."

## Blessings

I have never been asked to bless a computer yet, but I think it's only a matter of time. There is one church where I help out occasionally where I am asked to bless a pet rabbit every time I go there. The rabbit and I are becoming good friends, and as far as I can tell my blessings have not done him or his owner any harm!

Blessings have a variety of meanings in scripture. In the Hebrew Bible, where there are three words for various kinds of curses, there is only one word for "bless" or "blessing" — *berakah* — and its passive participle, *baruk*, meaning "blessed." Being blessed is the opposite of being cursed and includes such good things as health, vitality, fertility, peace, and long life. There is also a sense of "blessing" meaning "praise" or "thanksgiving" as in Psalm 34:1: "I will bless the LORD at all times; his praise shall continually be in my mouth."

In the New Testament Jesus commands his disciples not to curse (Luke 6:28), but blessings are frequent. One thinks immediately of the Beatitudes in Matthew's version of the Sermon on the Mount, and there is this in Ephesians 1:3:"Blessed be the God and Father of our Lord Jesus Christ, who has blessed us in Christ with every spiritual blessing in the heavenly places...." We also have, most importantly, the sanctification and dedication of bread and wine in, for example, Matthew 26:26 and Luke 24:30. The Greek word often translated as "blessed" also can mean "fortunate" or "happy" and can also mean "holy."

From ancient times blessings have been pronounced, and the church has taken it upon itself to authorize priests and bishops to pronounce special blessings as a way of engaging the church in a kind of "official" collective request to God for special favors and good things. These blessings range from that given to my friend the rabbit, to a congregation at the end of worship, to people who wish to ask God's favor upon their lifelong commitment to one another. George Councell, Episcopal bishop of New Jersey, once amused an assembly of priests in his diocese by telling them that as a young priest he had been given a copy of *A Manual for Priests* published by the Cowley Fathers that contained numerous forms of blessings, including one that soon became his favorite, titled, "The Blessing of Anything Whatsoever."[13]

A lovely way to employ blessings that helps unify a community is during the ministry's regular worship service to bless everyone having a birthday that month. At some appropriate time before, during, or at the end of the service everyone having a birthday that month can be invited to come forward, and some fitting prayer and blessing can be offered for them. At those colleges not in session over the summer, everyone with a summer birthday can be blessed during the month preceding or following the summer break.

The chaplain should be willing to pronounce the church's blessing whenever asked. College students often are in need of the reassurance and comfort a blessing pronounced by a priest can give, and some, owing to the tradition in which they were raised, attach special meaning to blessings given by priests and ministers. But in addition to those blessings that the church provides, there is a sense in which blessings are not the province only of priests and ministers. Anyone, for example, can offer a table blessing. Anyone can ask God's blessing on an undertaking such as a student group setting out to work on a Habitat for Humanity project. Anyone, in short, is empowered by God to bless anything (good) whatsoever.

If it is a goal of campus ministry to raise up young people as leaders for the church — and I think this is central to campus ministry — then every opportunity should be given to students to exercise a priestly function, albeit not in the same way as those who are ordained. Clericalism — an overemphasis on the ordained ministry — can, over time, rob the church of the rich gifts laypeople have to offer. The chief warrant for ministry is not ordination but baptism, and this should always be emphasized by the chaplain. A sensitive chaplain can and should maintain the prerogatives of the ordained without diminishing the ministry of those who are not called to ordination.

## Leading Prayer

As with blessings, every priest and minister has a story to tell about how, upon being ordained, he or she suddenly became the designated leader of all prayer. Invariably the only ordained person at a dinner party will be asked to give the table blessing. The ordained members of any committee or group associated with the church will always be expected to lead the others in the opening and closing prayers. Here again, the chaplain must exercise judgment and sensitivity. Sometimes, it is appropriate to lead the prayer, as when the members of the group are not known to one another and the ordained person is really the only logical choice for leading a prayer so as to avoid awkwardness. But in a group of people who meet regularly, such as a Bible study group or a confirmation class, taking turns leading prayer may be a way to enhance the reality of the ministry of all the baptized and the priesthood of all believers.

There are many excellent books of table blessings and other prayers that the chaplain can have on hand to offer to someone who is asked to lead a group in prayer. It is usually best to ask someone to lead prayer before the event so as to lessen the embarrassment of being put on the spot and to give the prayer leader time to prepare.

## Being a Model of a Prayerful Life

Notwithstanding the need to avoid being the only "designated prayer leader" on the scene, it is important for the chaplain as priest to be a guide for those who are inexperienced in prayer. One way to do this is to be faithful to one's own daily prayer life, something about which I will have more to say in the chapter on the chaplain as pilgrim. But for chaplains to be able readily to lead prayer in a spontaneous, unaffected manner, they need to be experienced and centered in the ways of prayer themselves. John Witherspoon, one of Princeton's early presidents and a signer of the Declaration of Independence, once said, "One of the most useful qualifications of a minister is that he have a lively sense of religion upon his own heart."

One way of being a model of a prayerful life is to insist on ending each pastoral care meeting with an individual or group with a brief prayer. Sometimes this seems natural as if the person is expecting just such an ending to a chat with a priest or minister. At other times, however, a student may be finished with whatever needed to be talked about and be ready to leave without a prayer. In those instances it may be a bit awkward to suggest ending with a prayer, but those instances might just be the ones where doing so is most important and will have the greatest impact. Such a prayer should be completely ad lib and collect up and offer to God all the concerns and worries just discussed in the meeting. The prayer might name the person, couple, or group and be as specific as possible to their concerns. It should also state a sense of confidence in God's love and mercy as a way of assuring the person that he or she is not alone in the world. An example of such a prayer might be:

O God, I thank you for bringing me together with Bill this afternoon and for the time we have had together. I ask you, Lord, to help Bill to see clearly your love for him and that the trouble he is having in completing his thesis is not a judgment upon him or a sign of your displeasure. Instead help him to see how these times may be a blessing for him, and that even in the midst of his deepest distress he may come to know that you are beside him as a friend and brother. Amen.

## Sacraments and Rituals

One of the great tragedies of the Protestant Reformation was a wholesale "throwing out the baby with the bath water" where sacraments and rituals were concerned. To be sure, there were many abuses and superstitions associated with the church's use of sacraments and rituals in the high medieval period that were sadly and desperately in need of reforming. But sacraments — defined as outward and visible signs of inward and spiritual grace — can be a powerful way for people to be assured of, and thus experience, God's love and grace in a personal way. Happily, there seems to be a recovery of ritual underway among many reformed Christians. The regular celebration of the Lord's Supper is very important to spiritual growth and to the building up of a community. Several other rituals can serve the same purpose.

One kind of ritual marks a transition in the life of the ministry. Each year when a new group of student leaders takes charge, the campus ministry can celebrate the new ministry within its main worship service of the week. Special prayers might be recited that commission new student leaders. This will have the effect of emphasizing the importance of their ministry as well as asking God's blessing upon it. In addition, it will cause the new leaders to be more mindful of the important office they are assuming and strengthen their resolve to be faithful to the demands and the serious responsibilities of the office.[14]

One of the most powerful rituals the church has to offer is the reconciliation of a penitent in a private ritual with a priest or minister. Commonly known as "confession," this ritual is often misunderstood and thus is not often used. But there are many people who, for a wide variety of reasons, do not feel they are worthy to take communion or who are having difficulty making progress in their spiritual lives — indeed, in their lives in general — owing to some terrible burden of guilt that they cannot lay down. A ritual reconciliation best follows a series of conversations between a chaplain and a person troubled by something past. In one instance in my own campus ministry a young man was troubled by his abuse of alcohol, which caused him to lash out at his girlfriend and to embarrass himself in front of many of his friends. In another, a young woman was plagued by the guilt associated with an eating disorder. And in yet another, a senior professor had lived for years with a yearning for an assurance of God's love and with the burden of feeling unworthy of it and had thus avoided taking communion. In each of these cases, a sacramental "confession" seemed appropriate in some holy place, like a chapel, with a solemn rehearsing of all the burdens and sources of guilt experienced by the penitent and the minister's ritual assurance of God's unequivocal and unconditional love, mercy, and forgiveness. These private, heart-wrenching rituals go beyond anything that can be experienced in public confessions of sin and assurance of forgiveness in the various Christian worship traditions. They are so powerful that they invariably end with both the minister and the penitent a bit teary-eyed, and with the penitent feeling almost giddy with relief and joy. Many traditions provide for this kind of reconciliation — Episcopal, Presbyterian, Roman Catholic, Orthodox — and some do not. However, some form of private reconciliation suitable to any Christian denomination can be developed and used to great effect by a sensitive chaplain.[15]

Life transitions are also occasions for rituals that are elevated in importance by their celebration by a priest or minister in the context of community worship. For example, a special form of prayer for the celebration of a dissertation defense or for a group of graduating seniors can be a way of employing ritual and the priestly function of a chaplain to build up the church and God's people. The commissioning and celebration of a new chaplain's ministry is another way to gather the community in prayer in the context of formal rituals where a larger gathering of students than is usual together with visiting chaplains and students from other denominations can be an occasion of great joy.

Finally, I would urge the chaplain as priest to consider it a part of the office of the chaplain to encourage young people to pursue a life of ministry, whether as a layperson or through ordination. I constantly remind Princeton students that just by the fact of their baptism, their attendance at worship, and their many intellectual gifts they are called to some kind of ministry. Their task is to discern, with God's help, what form that ministry will take.

An ordained chaplain of any tradition, whether called a "priest" or not, nonetheless engages in the priestly functions of leading worship, rituals, and prayers; of pronouncing blessings; and of assuring penitents of God's loving forgiveness. In exercising this holy function the chaplain as priest will be cautious about self-celebration and will center it in his or her own routine of daily prayer. And the chaplain as priest will be vigilant about the scriptural and theological foundations for these priestly functions, knowing that the "doing" of worship is a form of teaching others about the faith. This now leads us to a closer look at the teaching aspects of campus ministry as we turn to the role of chaplain as rabbi.

# Chapter 3

# The Chaplain as Rabbi

*A scholar qualified to teach the law of God; a teacher.*

———— ✠ ————

A T THE BEGINNING of each academic year, the Roman Catholic chaplain at Princeton hosts a gathering of all denominational chaplains and deans of the Office of Religious Life. It is a time for newcomers to be introduced and for everyone to share a bit about their summer and their plans for the coming year. Mostly it is a time of fellowship among colleagues who work well together and are fond of one another.

One year the senior rabbi brought along his new associate, a young Orthodox rabbi named Uri Cohen. As was our usual custom, we went around the room introducing ourselves. It is usually strictly a case of "name, rank, and serial number" — "Hi, everyone! I'm Steve White, the Episcopal chaplain. Had a good summer. Glad to see you all here. I'm looking forward to another busy year working with you." — that sort of thing.

When we got to Uri he flashed a big smile and introduced himself. Then he said, without skipping a beat, "Uri is short for Uriel, who was one of the archangels. It means 'God is the dispenser of beloved warmth' or 'God is my fire,' which I prefer. I'm really looking forward to working with all of you." He said all this in the most matter-of-fact and engaging way without a trace of the pedantic or of condescension.

I found Uri's introduction delightfully different, and my immediate thought was, "This guy is a natural teacher." It almost seemed as if either by temperament or training, or both, he is hard-wired to seize every opportunity to impart information and knowledge to others. And he does this in a way that draws people in and makes them eager for more. What a gift! What an example! What a rabbi!

The use of the term "rabbi" with reference to a Christian minister may at first seem odd to some. I acknowledge that I am borrowing the term from Judaism, and I do so because I think the Jews have preserved a great tradition of study and learning coupled with an imperative to teach that is very rich indeed. Jewish rabbis — ancient and modern — have much to teach us about how to engage our minds in probing God's truths and about how to share learning within the community. So it is with a grateful heart that I use this term, which was, of course, applied to Jesus himself.

Campus ministers are called to be teachers — to be rabbis. Most of us are not, however, called to be teachers in the same sense as those who are faculty members who teach courses. Our teaching is always theocentric, always searching for ways to proclaim the gospel, to make God known, to point to the connection of the reality of God with all other fields of knowledge. It is more about enabling people to find God than it is about simply imparting information, although there is an element of that too, as, for example, when you are asked to explain a doctrine, a ritual, or the church's position on a moral issue.

## Equipping (the Saints)

Everyone is called to ministry by virtue of baptism. I think the ante is raised considerably when the baptized have enjoyed the benefits of a college education and perhaps graduate school. Well-educated people are by definition called upon to be leaders in all aspects of the life of a community. At Princeton I really push hard on this issue by pointing out that by virtue of receiving such a good education and by choosing to be active in the church, our students are "on the hook" to serve the church as leaders, both now and in the future.

A good general education may equip people for leadership, but not necessarily for ministry. For that, the saints — those sanctified by baptism — must be prepared with what we might call theoretical as well as practical knowledge. A great deal of this theoretical and practical knowledge is gained by integrating all the knowledge and skills acquired in classes and other activities with a very focused and intentional program of Christian education in the chaplaincy. Thus, for the chaplain as rabbi, every moment must be thought of, and seized, as a teaching moment. The way that liturgy is celebrated, the content of sermons, the resources on a Web site, formal and informal conversations, pastoral counseling, opportunities for outreach service, as well as Bible study and confirmation classes are all opportunities to impart, implicitly or explicitly, what it is to be a disciple of Jesus Christ in the world.

In other words, it is not enough simply to deliver food to the poor or visit with the elderly in a nursing home. Social workers do that and are trained to do it well. We do such things as an expression of our wish to serve others in love through Jesus Christ, to love others as God loves us. We help build a house or deliver food not for some faceless and nameless poor person, but for Jesus Christ himself. This simple, straightforward idea cannot be taken for granted. The chaplain cannot assume that everyone is clear about why a Christian chaplaincy would sponsor such activities; the chaplain must *say* why it is done and say that it is done in the name of Jesus Christ. Beginning the visit to the nursing home or the housing project with a prayer is necessary to this, but not sufficient.

The prayer can be a way of beginning the conversation about why we do good works. I won't engage in a debate here about works righteousness versus a motivation to serve that emanates from our gratitude for God's immeasurable grace freely given. In either case, whatever one's theology is about what motivates us to do good works, we must, as chaplains, make the theology and the motivation explicit so that the service project becomes an extracurricular activity that not only benefits those whom we serve, but equips the saints for leadership in the church. It's a two-for-one proposition.

This issue highlights the difference between a college chaplaincy and a high school youth group. Students often come to college with beliefs and attitudes about God, the Bible, and their own relationship (and that of others) to God that are "freeze dried" at the sixth-grade level. They may be firmly held, but they are usually largely unexamined and often prone to fracture under stress. As the writer of Ephesians says, "We must no longer be children, tossed to and fro and blown about by every wind of doctrine" (4:14). College is a time to take the beliefs we have acquired as children and unpack them, examine them, and evaluate them. It is a time when beliefs may shift as a result of closely examining them. And it is a time of coming to a place where, having questioned and examined attitudes and beliefs, we are strengthened in our faith and in our commitment to Christ. At least that's how it's supposed to work!

Chaplains are always eager for new recruits who come from strong high school Christian youth groups. These are the young people who are committed and "fired up" and who are a bit more comfortable with talking about their faith. In these cases it is often easy for the chaplain to assume that the faith of these young people is tried and true, and just as often, this is a mistake. The faith we see in the youth group veterans is usually broad but not very deep (there are, happily, many exceptions). It also is often very brittle. Shallow, brittle faith does not do very well under pressure, especially the kind of pressures one experiences in college and later in life.

The chaplain as rabbi can play a key role in deepening students' faith by seizing every opportunity that presents itself to explain, elaborate, and gently challenge particular beliefs. By doing this the chaplain not only teaches, but models a healthy intellectual engagement with scripture and the traditions of the church that can result in a more robust faith that will more readily withstand the inevitable storms of life.

The imperative to teach in order to equip the saints relates to the imperative to create an environment of questioning everything.

Everything must be on the table to be examined. This poses a particular challenge for some Christian traditions. Those traditions that embrace biblical inerrancy are limited in their questioning by an underlying belief that the Bible is what it is and cannot be questioned or challenged in any way. So, for example, a student who has been exposed to higher biblical criticism and questions the authorship of Ephesians will be summarily referred to Ephesians 3:1: "This is the reason that *I Paul* am a prisoner for Christ Jesus...," which settles the issue without further discussion. Any tradition that locates authority in only one place will have trouble with this idea. A student I worked with ran into this very problem as a leader in an evangelical Bible study group. While studying Ephesians he noticed something his friends thought he shouldn't have noticed, namely, that the literary style of Ephesians is different from known Pauline texts like Romans and 1 Corinthians. When his further study led him to raise the authorship of Ephesians as a discussion point, he was promptly asked to leave the group. Happily, we were able to welcome him into our group, where he freely pursued his interest in close readings of scripture.

I recently heard another story about a Bible study group sponsored by an evangelical group on an Ivy League campus in which the student group leader asserted that a certain New Testament passage was one long sentence, and the leader attached great importance to that seemingly irrefutable fact. Another student then pointed out that the original Greek manuscripts had neither punctuation nor capitalization and that later translators added the punctuation long after the original was written. When the latter student pressed his point, he was asked to leave the group.

Similarly, the Roman Catholic Church forbids debate about certain topics in formal church-sponsored forums. A notable and problematic example for many students is the issue of the ordination of women to the priesthood. When devout Roman Catholic women feel a call to the priesthood and wish to have a group discussion on the

subject led by a priest, the chaplain is in a difficult position with regard to church law and must decide whether or not to engage the
issue publicly. If he chooses not to, then the women — and men! —
who are troubled by this issue must accommodate their questioning,
and their disagreement, with their intense desire to remain faithful
to the teaching of their church. But, with regard to the subject before us — the equipping of the saints — an opportunity to engage an
issue thoroughly is short-circuited by a competing, and in this case
overriding, requirement. In these cases the chaplain will try to find
ways to instruct students on the background and reasoning behind
the church's teaching.

In the spirit of "speaking the truth in love" (Eph. 4:15) to my
evangelical and Roman Catholic brothers and sisters, I would suggest
that Christ's church will be most robust and most able to spread the
gospel when all its ministers — and that, of course, means everyone —
have done the hard work to understand thoroughly what they believe
and why. Challenging underlying beliefs and assumptions is a healthy
and necessary part of this process upon which all good teaching rests.

## Thinking Theologically

During the autumn of 2003 following the election, consent, and
consecration of the Rev. Gene Robinson — a gay man living in a
long-term relationship with another man — as Episcopal bishop of
New Hampshire and all the controversy that ensued, I participated
in several conversations with colleagues and friends on both sides of
the human sexuality debate within the Anglican Communion who
lamented the poverty of the theological discussion surrounding the
issue. I have heard similar observations from Methodists, Presbyterians, and others, and I tend to agree that we could be having a much
more sophisticated theological discussion about this and many other
subjects than we usually have.

To put the matter in an admittedly overly simplistic way, those
on the so-called liberal or progressive side of the human sexuality

debate seem to rely on pastoral concerns and concerns for equity
and justice, while those on the opposing side — whether you call
them conservatives or traditionalists — seem to rely principally on
scriptural arguments to support their views. To be sure, the human
sexuality controversy is much more complicated than this, and it
*should* concern itself with pastoral, equity, justice, and scriptural concerns. But there is a lot more territory to cover than this, and I believe
the activists on both sides of this controversy have missed an opportunity to delve into this issue in a theologically profound way. Put
another way, to think theologically about an issue such as this it is
necessary, but not sufficient, to think pastorally and scripturally.

This issue concerns not just professional theologians: it concerns
everyone. Just as every baptized person is a minister, every baptized
person is also a theologian. And if the church must prepare the faithful to be ministers, so must it prepare them to be theologians. We have
not done well in this area at any level of the church — nationally or
locally. As noted elsewhere in this book, young people are woefully
illiterate with regard to scripture and basic Christian traditions and
beliefs, even those who had a perfect attendance record at Sunday
school. Campus ministries are perhaps a place where leaders of the
future church can be educated about how to go beyond facile and
simplistic arguments that support strongly held opinions to a place
where deliberations about mission and morality are marked by nu-
anced conversations that employ the full range of scripture, tradition,
experience, and reason. This, of course, is tricky. How does one exercise a ministry that is prophetic and yet also encourages people of
differing views to come together to work carefully through a complicated range of issues in order to arrive at a moral position that satisfies
the test of theological rigor? Must the chaplain as rabbi remain neutral on every issue so as to allow space for students to grapple with
those issues themselves, uncontaminated by the views of the chaplain? Is the role of the chaplain as rabbi to teach students whatever it
takes to get them to come around to his or her own position, or is it

the chaplain's role to help them arrive at their own position, whatever it may end up being, by taking a well-thought-out path?

I believe the answer to these last two questions is that the chaplain as rabbi must remain neutral and not enforce his/her own position, yet must assist students in discovering and appropriating for themselves their own understandings. It is an inherent part of the role of chaplain as rabbi (and as prophet) to be very clear about his or her own views on moral issues. Failing to be forthright about views will compromise one's integrity and credibility. And it is probably impossible to remain totally poker-faced about one's views anyway. But being clear about them requires the chaplain to make sure a respect for differing views is conveyed just as clearly. Being nasty is not the same as being forthright. Agreement and respect are not the same thing, and being nasty and conveying disrespect for the views of another, especially while pretending not to, is the best way I know of shutting down a productive dialog.

The chaplain as rabbi will assure that the chaplaincy ends up preaching to the choir if it becomes known that there is no tolerance for differing views and if the chaplain's agenda is seen to be force-fitting everyone's views to his or her own. There are certain issues, to be sure, where there is no room to budge — anti-Semitism and racism, for example. But there are many other issues where faithful, prayerful Christians will disagree and the Holy Spirit's will can only be discerned by a genuine openness to all views until some kind of godly resolution can be reached — and that can take time. For a Christian minister, browbeating is no substitute for discernment in community.

I think many liberal or progressive people believe that if others would just think through complex issues they would become liberals too. And I think conservatives or traditionalists believe that if people just read their Bibles and honored the ancient traditions of the church, moral choices would be self-evident. These attitudes inform two different approaches to an impoverished substitute for theological conversations in the church. Chaplains who take their role as rabbi seriously are troubled by this. It is beyond the scope of this book to delve too deeply into theological method, but I do think it is important to sketch out an approach that might best facilitate doing real theology rather than an approach that employs scripture and pastoral concerns as brickbats.[16]

I want first to say a word — and just a word — about the authority of scripture as a basis for doing theological discernment. While I believe that "Holy Scripture containeth all things necessary to salvation,"[17] I also believe that "We understand the meaning of the Bible by the help of the Holy Spirit, who guides the Church in the true interpretation of the Scriptures."[18] In other words, the scriptures guide us, but collectively, as the church, we must interpret their meaning; we cannot accept each passage of scripture out of context as meaning something that it may or may not mean.[19] Before even embarking upon a theological inquiry into a moral issue, it might be profitable to study the Bible from the thirty-thousand-foot level, so to speak, to help students discover a shift that Jews and Christians make from a fulfillment of the self in the Hellenistic mind-set to the "other" in the Bible. Indeed, even in the Bible itself this shift can be noticed. It is important to note this shift before doing any serious work in Christian moral theology. Appendix 3 provides a suggested outline for a study of the Bible in which this shift can be noticed, for which resource I am grateful to Thomas Breidenthal, dean of religious life at Princeton.

We do not begin our approach with generalities. We must break the issue down. For instance, we must ask what is the inherent tendency of the act under consideration — not its motivation, but its effect?

Consider a young person's decision to have sex. Thomas Aquinas said when we are trying to determine whether something is right or wrong we must to try to ferret out its ultimate object. He said we must avoid thinking of the *consequences* of the act that may cloud our judgment owing to our self-interest. An act may be evil even though the consequences may seem to be good. When presented with an issue, we must not try to resolve it quickly, but enter into its parts and components to show how *all* sides relate to the Christian faith. We must ask what is at stake in the church — the community — in terms of ultimate things. In other words, the conversation tries to consider where we are going — i.e., toward God — and where the act under consideration is going, what its ultimate end is, and thus whether it may take us closer to God or further away from God. Is the desire for sex centered in the self? Or is it centered in concern for and love of the "other" — that is, in the unselfish, Christ-like "love of neighbor"? What seems like a simple choice suddenly becomes rather more complicated when thought of this way.

A middle way between complete reliance on the Bible and a reliance on a set of prescribed rules is an approach to moral issues worth teaching university students about. Such an approach to moral theology has tended over the centuries to subordinate specific policies and rules to a broader focus on general principles. Biblical foundations should never be dismissed out of hand, but neither should we neglect the reality that Christian life evolves in a complex and confusing way. Thus, Christian moral theology is at its best when it seeks to solve particular moral questions in the broadest possible context of biblical foundations, tradition, new scientific discoveries, collective experience, and the moral tendencies of each act.[20]

Preparing students to think through these issues in this way will necessitate avoiding the temptation to jump right into a hot controversy without, for example, making sure the group knows something about how to interpret scripture, how to consider the traditional views of the church through history, and something about the realities of how God's will might be revealed to us through science and through an understanding of the lives of others in our own day. Students who are required, for example, to take *basic* courses in biology and chemistry before embarking upon independent study in genomics will readily grasp the necessity of doing this. The task of the chaplain as rabbi, in other words, is not to *settle* controversial issues, but to *equip* students with the theological tools with which they can settle the issues for themselves for the rest of their lives — or at least to begin that educational process.

## Classes and Groups

I said earlier that every moment of interaction between the chaplain as rabbi and students is a teaching moment. But it is equally true that some kinds of teaching require a bit more focus, time, and energy than a passing explanation or a quick conversation. Experience shows that many college students who are drawn to religious fellowships are hungry for what they cannot get anywhere else on campus, namely, instruction in the faith in the company of others seeking the same thing. Evangelical groups are expert at capitalizing on this hunger by being on the scene early in each term with opportunities to sign up for Bible study groups. The hunger of some students for instruction in the faith will cause them to drift toward evangelical circles if they sense that there are no other opportunities for learning about Christianity. Indeed, we owe a debt of gratitude to evangelical groups on campus for the attention they have given to Bible study. This then is a challenge for all campus ministries: to serve up a variety of opportunities as early as possible each term for students to learn the basics about the Christian faith in a way that allows them to question, doubt, and debate the issues.

Campus ministries can employ a variety of didactic groups to satisfy the demand for instruction. So-called seeker's groups or inquirer's classes can be offered for those who are just beginning to explore Christianity. They can focus on a study of a particular Gospel or upon basic Christian doctrines. One approach might be a brief course that unpacks and analyzes the doctrines contained in the Nicene Creed or explores the doctrine of the Trinity, or of how the doctrine of the incarnation is related to the doctrine of the atonement.

Another is to focus on the rite for the sacrament of Baptism in the group's book of worship, such as the Presbyterian *Book of Common Worship* or the Episcopal *Book of Common Prayer.* Such an exercise

could be based on the ancient dictum of *lex orandi, lex credendi* —
what we pray is what we believe, and what we believe is what we
pray — and could culminate with a reaffirmation of baptismal vows.
A similar approach could be taken with the service of Holy Eucharist
so that the meaning of the words and gestures associated with this
sacrament are fully examined, understood, and thus more spiritually
powerful. This can easily be done by printing out the entire service in
two columns with brief explanatory notes in the right-hand column.

In addition to inquirer's classes or classes focused on specific aspects of the faith, more systematic and thorough instruction in the
faith can be offered in prebaptismal and preconfirmation classes. For
very small campus ministry groups, these two can be combined, and
in parish settings students can join with adults seeking confirmation
or baptism. In these groups it is usually a good idea to create a covenant among the participants that binds them to one another in a
promise of regular attendance, mutual prayer, and confidentiality.

There are two general introductions to Christianity that hold great
promise for evangelizing the unchurched and for educating those who
may have been brought up in the church but whose understanding of
the faith is incomplete. One is Charles Marnham and Nikki Gumbel's
Alpha course developed at Holy Trinity, Brompton, an evangelical
Anglican church in a fashionable section of London. It is a fifteen-
session course based on a simple format of gathering for supper, a
video presentation and talk, and a small group session designed to
facilitate discussion of the material. The sessions begin and end with
prayer, and at the end of the course there is a retreat. The talk titles
are:[21]

- Christianity: Boring, Untrue and Irrelevant?
- Who Is Jesus?
- Why Did Jesus Die?
- How Can I Be Sure of My Faith?
- Why and How Should I Read the Bible?

◆ Why and How Do I Pray?

◆ How Does God Guide Us?

◆ Who Is the Holy Spirit?

◆ What Does the Holy Spirit Do?

◆ How Can I Be Filled with the Spirit?

◆ How Can I Resist Evil?

◆ Why and How Should We Tell Others?

◆ Does God Heal Today?

◆ What About the Church?

◆ How Can I Make the Most of the Rest of My Life?

The Alpha course has been extremely popular among a number of denominations in Britain and the United States, and it can easily be adapted for use on campus. One criticism from some quarters is that the course's theology is conservative, which has caused some to adapt the course so as to eliminate portions that do not fit the particular theology of the group offering the course. Another course is "Via Media," which was developed by an Episcopal Church group in the United States. Modeled on the Alpha concept, it has a decidedly more progressive stance and covers its material in seven sessions followed by a retreat with the following titles:[22]

◆ Via Media: An Anglican Way of Being Christian

◆ God and Creation: The Abundance of God's Goodness

◆ God in Jesus: An Incarnational Faith

◆ God the Holy Spirit: The Breath of New Life

◆ The Bible: The Word of God for the People of God

◆ Sin: Roadblocks to Abundant Life

◆ Thy Kingdom Come: The Promise of Christian Hope

◆ Retreat: So, What?

The Via Media course also includes table fellowship, video presentations, small groups, and prayer. Both Alpha and Via Media are excellent resources not only for student populations but also for the entire university community, including faculty and staff. One will need to judge how each program suits the theology the campus ministry wishes to embrace, realizing that any program is likely to deviate to some degree from what one might view as an ideal. If one way of thinking of an ideal is traditional, orthodox Christianity as defined in chapter 2, and if that is thought of as the center of a spectrum, then one might find Via Media rather more left of center and Alpha as right of center. And these courses are decidedly not mutually exclusive; a group could use both to good effect.

Bible study groups offer many possibilities for Christian education. It will often come as a shock for students to discover that there is not one story of creation in Genesis, but two, or that the four Gospels do not agree on all details of the passion and death of Jesus, or that all four do not include stories about Jesus' birth. More sophisticated groups will enjoy discussing the clear stylistic differences between the Letter to the Ephesians and Pauline letters such as Romans, Galatians, and Philemon. Did Paul actually write Ephesians? If not, how do we deal with statements in the letter (1:1 and 3:1) that seem to identify the letter as authored by Paul? In the same vein an examination of the various prohibitions of the holiness code in Leviticus will result in a lively discussion. These examinations can, in turn, lead to discussions concerning the authority of the Bible and how it may guide us in our lives, especially when the advice in the Bible is internally inconsistent or runs counter to beliefs we have derived from other sources, such as the church's tradition and our own reason and experience.

In all these groups the chaplain as rabbi is a key player. The chaplain's training, experience, and expertise is a valuable resource for the groups, and the groups offer the chaplain an opportunity to teach. Even the brightest university students often have large lacunae in their understanding of the nuances and complexities of theology, not to mention their biblical illiteracy. Nonetheless, these groups also challenge the chaplain as rabbi to find ways to draw students out in discussions that may be more profitable to their learning than simply lecturing.

## Calling versus Career: What's the Difference?

One of the issues that students perennially raise in campus ministries is how to discern the difference between a career and a true calling or vocation. Often this issue is dealt with in terms of a calling to ordained ministry versus other careers or callings. In the late 1940s and early 1950s the Episcopal chaplains at Princeton regularly invited to dinner at a chaplain's home students who were, however remotely, considering ordained ministry as a vocation. These groups were modeled on the mentoring groups offered by the university to students who wished to pursue careers in medicine or the law and, in the tradition of "pre-med" and "pre-law," this group was called "Pre-Theo." There are no precise records of how many members of these groups ever went on to seminary, but we know there were quite a few. Indeed, a whole generation of the church's leadership was raised up in groups like this, which flourished around the country during that period. With the decline in campus ministries of the late 1960s and early 1970s, out went the Pre-Theo groups and along with them went future crops of potential ordained leaders in the church. So today we find ourselves with a dearth of ordained leaders under the age of thirty-five.

Shortly after I stumbled upon a mention of Princeton's Pre-Theo group in some old files, I put the following notice in a Sunday service bulletin:

> Have you ever thought of becoming a priest? It's a wonderful life if that's what God is calling you to. Pray about it, talk with family and friends about it, and talk to a priest. You may be glad you did!

I included this notice frankly because I needed to fill up some space and didn't have anything else to put in. I was astounded that within a couple of weeks six students approached me to discuss a call to ordained ministry. This led to a revival of the Pre-Theo group, and it is still going strong, meeting monthly for Sunday dinners at the chaplain's house just as it did over half a century ago.

These groups that explore the whole question of how God calls people to ordained ministry and how a calling is different from a career can be modified to include a broader audience of students. Recruiters from banks, investment brokerage firms, the military, consulting firms, and many other fields swarm over college campuses luring the "best and the brightest" with high pay and high adventure and often dodge the issue of what a person truly feels called to do in life by his or her deepest yearnings. Family and friends will often conspire with such recruiters and in effect be the voice of the serpent when they say things like, "Why would you want to waste your good education on being a teacher [or priest, artist, dancer, social worker, etc.]?" The chaplain as rabbi must be in a position to help students think through the differences between a career and a calling, beginning with the warning that all callings can be careers, but not all careers are callings, and that it is important and legitimate to follow your heart as well as your head.[23] And the chaplain will not want to limit the scope of this issue only to ordained ministry.

The table on the following page can be the basis of a very fruitful discussion on this subject.[24] After distributing the table to the group, a few general statements can be made and questions posed. What is the difference between a career and a calling? Well, first of all, a calling is from God and its ultimate goal is God. Not all careers are callings, but they can be. A career — whether it's medicine, engineering, finance, or public safety — *can* be a calling from God just as ordained ministry can be. How can you tell the difference? Then the group can begin working its way through the table. I can promise you this: the conversation will not lag, and it will not be boring!

| In a Career you... | In a Calling you... |
|---|---|
| ...seek to be successful. | ...seek to be valuable. |
| ...look out for yourself. | ...look after others. |
| ...ask how to get from "here" to "there" (focus on destination). | ...ask whether going "there" is worth it (focus on the journey). |
| ...seek to make money. | ...seek to make a difference rather than money. |
| ...seek to be powerful. | ...seek to lift up and protect the powerless. |
| ...are detached from your deepest longings. | ...heed your deepest longings. |
| ...expend maximum input and achieve minimal results. | ...achieve maximum results with minimal input (not *always* true, but usually is). |
| ...experience more stress than fun. | ...have lots of fun even when stressed. |
| ...have a compartmentalized life. | ...live an integrated life. |
| ...live a life alien to your identity. | ...live a life congruent with your identity. |
| ...enjoy lots of pleasure (money, power, etc.); not much happiness. | ...experience true happiness even when things may be unpleasant. |
| ...believe you are the center of the universe. | ...*know* that God is the center of the universe. |

## Individual Direction and Mentoring

Thus far we have been looking at the rabbinical role of the chaplain in group settings. Sometimes the role of chaplain as rabbi can entail working with individual students as a spiritual director or as a mentor. This can be a fascinating and multifaceted experience for both the chaplain and the student, entailing, as it does, aspects of wise sage, friend, prodder, spiritual companion, and cheerleader. There are times when the conversations can plumb the depths of the soul and other times, even with the same student, when the conversation is amazingly simple-minded but no less important — such as harping on a student to write two pages a day for a month in order to get a senior thesis completed on time.

It is one of the many oddities of late adolescence that a young person who will scorn and reject any advice from a loving parent will eagerly listen to a chaplain of the same age as the parent for any advice and wisdom the chaplain wishes to impart. Indeed, it was amusing — and, to be honest, quite comforting — to see my own college-age daughter scoff at my advice while her contemporaries at Princeton — who scoffed at their own parents' advice — sought mine. This is to be expected. Bright young people are perfectly aware that older people have experience and knowledge they do not possess and are usually eager to learn from it. But owing to the need for people in late adolescence to establish independence from their parents, it is usually the case that seeking advice and help from parents is fraught with tension. This places the chaplain as rabbi in a position to be a mentor and a guide through the shoals of choosing a major field of study, a career, a life partner, or even a summer job. Such mentoring relationships can generate great affection and warmth between the student and the chaplain. This is certainly a good thing and can result in a relationship that lasts for years after the student leaves the university. But the closeness of the relationship may also give rise to the potential for violations of personal — even sexual — boundaries about which the chaplain must constantly be aware. I have more to say on this in the chapter on chaplain as pilgrim.

Teaching students the basics of the faith, helping them to appreciate what the Bible is — and is not — as a foundational, God-inspired document for us, and creating an environment where questioning can lead to new discoveries of how God works in the world and in each of us are ways the chaplain fulfills a rabbinical ministry on the campus. This leads us directly to our next topic regarding prophecy. In the next chapter we examine how the teaching function of the chaplain relates to the chaplain's prophetic function.

# Chapter 4

# The Chaplain as Prophet

*One who speaks for God and interprets God's will.*

———— ✠ ————

W ILLIAM SLOANE COFFIN, former chaplain at Yale University and at Williams College, was tireless in his public opposition to racism, the Vietnam War, and injustice wherever he found it, and he became a role model for a whole generation of prophetic campus ministers.

Unfortunately, those campus ministers who spoke out against the establishment in the late 1960s and the 1970s incurred the wrath of the establishment and suffered the consequences. It is probably no small coincidence that many of the mainline churches began to cut funding for campus ministries at the very time when campus chaplains were speaking out most forcefully against an unjust war in southeast Asia and for a radical inclusion of women, people of color, and other minorities in the mainstream of society. A similar backlash against prophetic voices on European campuses occurred there as well. We recall that there were plots against Jeremiah and that Amos was banished from the royal court. In our own time Dietrich Bonhoeffer, Martin Luther King Jr., and Oscar Romero were martyred, and Desmond Tutu, notwithstanding his Nobel Peace Prize and celebrity status, suffered many hardships resulting from his prominent opposition to apartheid in South Africa.

The consequences of being a prophet are profound. Unfortunately, contemplating these consequences constrains our willingness to engage the issues of the day prophetically. Sometimes the costs are dramatic and predictable — the loss of a job or the loss of the university's support for ministry. At other times the costs are subtle, may only be comprehended well after the fact, and can come not only from the establishment, but also from the very students themselves.

In the 1960s and 1970s college chaplains were, in a way, stepping out to lead a parade that had already begun, and that parade consisted of energized, politicized, and outraged students. Times have changed, and students today are generally much less willing to protest against the establishment than their parents' generation was. Indeed, it might even be said that there is a profound lack of collective outrage at the world's injustices. Thus, in a sense, there is not much of a parade to lead, and starting a parade is a formidable task if the potential marchers are not very interested in the cause, whatever it may be.

Yet there is no lack of issues that demand attention from Christian prophets. As I write this the United States is in its third year in a war in Iraq that has dubious origins and a dubious rationale. At home the health-care system is in shambles, and more and more children than ever live in poverty. Special-interest lobbies block efforts in the Congress to remove guns from the streets, and government seems to be retreating from many environmental gains made in the 1970s and 1980s. Racism and homophobia spark hate crimes around the country with alarming regularity. Hardly anyone can get by on a minimum-wage salary. There are always issues that need prophetic response.

Some of these issues that call for a Christian witness are not so much global as local, indeed as local as the campus itself. Yale University has recently been troubled by public demonstrations regarding pay and benefits for nonfaculty workers, which include graduate student teaching assistants. Princeton University's service workers have been supported by a small group of activist students who are concerned about their wage and benefit levels. Some religious leaders on campus were involved in this effort, which resulted in some very positive changes for the lowest-paid workers at the university.

Apart from the global and national issues and local issues that touch the lives of members of the campus community, there are, on most campuses, endemic evils that we might call "The Big Five" — attitudes and behaviors that are pernicious and that, in their fullest expression, explicitly or implicitly violate Jesus' commandment that we love our neighbor as ourselves. The Big Five are:

◆ Alcohol abuse (and abuse of other substances)

◆ Misogyny — the degradation of women

◆ Xenophobia — prejudice against "outsiders," however they are defined

◆ Homophobia

◆ Racism

Examples of each of the Big Five abuses can be found with alarming frequency in editorials and letters in student newspapers, posters around campus, party-time activities, the initiation practices of fraternities and sororities, class discussions, and institutional policies. Sometimes these issues intersect and overlap with issues in the larger society, and sometimes they are peculiar to a particular campus at a particular time. But they all demand a response that is rooted in a theology of Christ-centered justice — a justice based on unconditional love for the other. Because a response may not readily be forthcoming from the general community, a singular prophetic voice may be necessary first simply to name the evil and then to call others to resist it.

Several American colleges and universities embrace a tradition on April 24 called "Newman's Day," which involves each participant drinking a case of beer (twenty-four cans or bottles) over a twenty-four-hour period — with predictable results. This is based on the wholly apocryphal (and ludicrous) story of actor Paul Newman having once said in a speech, "Twenty-four hours in a day, twenty-four beers in a case. Coincidence? I think not." Each year this self-degrading behavior results in all the expectable displays of public drunkenness, including such behavior in class, as well as serious medical consequences including alcohol toxicity, injuries from falls, and unwanted sexual advances.

One year the Episcopal Church at Princeton University explored the notion of a preemptive response to "Newman's Day." Several options were discussed including posters, sermons, public forums, and so on. The approach that was finally settled on was the following full-page advertisement in the student newspaper, which two other religious organizations cosponsored:

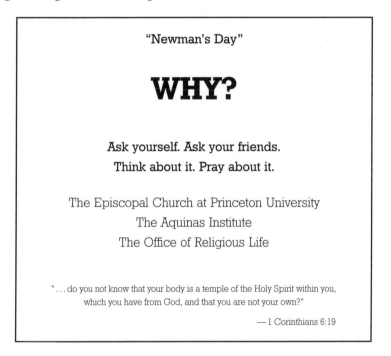

"Newman's Day"

# WHY?

**Ask yourself. Ask your friends.
Think about it. Pray about it.**

The Episcopal Church at Princeton University
The Aquinas Institute
The Office of Religious Life

" . . . do you not know that your body is a temple of the Holy Spirit within you,
which you have from God, and that you are not your own?"

— 1 Corinthians 6:19

The ad was well received by many on campus and even resulted in a story in the *New York Times* and other news outlets around the world.[25] What was most interesting, however, was the discussion leading up to the decision to run the ad. One former student leader of the group wrote in an e-mail: "I agree that we have to be careful not to offend anyone with the ads, especially the people who come to church events who also participate in Newman's Day. We don't want people to feel ashamed or reluctant to go to Episcopal services because they drink a lot (or even a little)." There were several others who expressed a similar opinion. This line of thinking was countered by the prevailing opinion best summarized in an e-mail from another student leader: "I don't think the fear of controversy should totally silence us at all. There are, on a number of issues, some rather unpleasant but necessary things that can and, from our point of view, should be said. Newman's Day raises the issue of alcohol abuse in general as well as the abuse of other substances. Certainly, these are not easy things for us to talk about, but I believe we need to have the courage to discuss them. We should be aware of such things and, consistent with our faith, be willing to question the status quo."

In this instance I had been making it clear for an entire year that I intended to be sure that the Episcopal Church at Princeton University would take some sort of public position against "Newman's Day." The students on their own might not have acted, and the chaplain's insistence that some prophetic response be made led to a thoughtful and, in the end, very effective witness. What is important here is not even so much the subject matter but the process that the student group went through with the chaplain to identify a wrong, to decide to speak out against it, and to determine the best way to proceed. It was done prayerfully and with input from a wide cross-section of students involved in the leadership of the ministry. This exercise relates to a topic that is admittedly small potatoes compared with issues such as intolerance and unjust war. But if a Christian campus ministry is, as I have suggested elsewhere, a school for ministry and a means by which the church "equips the saints," then it might be a means by which students are sensitized to the imperative for all Christians to be aware of any evil in the world around them and of the need to respond.

Perhaps the most important outcome of such an exercise is to expose our reluctance to rock the boat, a reluctance that seems to be particularly strong if the resistance to a prophetic stance comes not from outside the group, but from within. During the months preceding the invasion of Iraq in 2003 many campus religious groups discussed just war theory and the political as well as moral questions related to the impending and seemingly inevitable invasion. Very few religious groups and chaplains spoke out forcefully against the war. To some degree the inertia might have had to do with the wish not to alienate active members of the various religious groups who favored the invasion and who were perhaps in the majority among their coreligionists. Speaking truth to power is one thing if all that power is located outside the religious community and quite another when some of the power's allies and advocates are solidly within the community. When I suggested a response to Newman's Day or to the Iraq invasion some students who agreed with my underlying position on each issue opposed being too outspoken about both issues because they feared doing so would simply have the unintended effect of hardening the views of those who supported Newman's Day or the war.

This problem raises questions about how a campus religious community can best address one of the hottest issues facing most mainline denominations and one that is increasingly discussed in campus discussions, namely, the issue of homosexuality. One approach, informed by what we might call social justice concerns, might involve a chaplain being solidly in the camp of those who advocate same-sex unions and the ordination of openly gay persons. Such a chaplain might seek out opportunities to speak publicly about these issues and might organize study groups and forums to raise the group's consciousness about ways of reading the Bible that allow for committed, faithful, monogamous relationships between two persons of the same gender. Such an approach might over time lead to gay, lesbian, bisexual, and transgender students finding a spiritual home in such a chaplaincy, whereas those who are opposed to the views expressed by this approach might feel alienated.

A traditionalist approach, by contrast, would cause the chaplain to be public and visible on campus in expressing the view that while homosexual persons are to be loved and treated with the same respect and dignity as anyone else, sex between those of the same gender is contrary to a faithful Christian reading of scripture and contrary to long-standing Christian tradition. As with the social justice approach, the chaplain might organize opportunities for the issue to be discussed and studied in light of the point of view that he or she holds and, as with the other approach, like-minded people would be expected to participate in all aspects of the chaplaincy's common life in greater numbers than those who hold differing views.

The challenge here (and with other similarly controversial issues such as the ordination of women, war in Iraq, and so on) is how to both take a prophetic stance and assure people with differing views that we can pray and share a common life together. It is indeed a challenge for the whole Christian church to learn how to remain in community in the midst of gut-wrenching controversy when the proponents of each point of view are good, decent, prayerful, faithful Christians.

The competing "goods" in this scenario are both valuable: the prophetic integrity of the chaplain on the one hand, and the preservation of the community on the other. A vociferously prophetic chaplain runs the risk of alienating some members of the community with whom he or she disagrees. A silent chaplain preserves the community at the risk of compromising his or her prophetic sense of right and wrong and could be accused of having a lack of nerve and of being unfaithful to the Gospels. A hard choice, this!

Rabbi Stephen S. Wise, writing in the *New York Times* in 1906, gave a principled and honorable answer to this dilemma: "The chief office of the minister, I take it, is not to represent the views of the congregation, but to proclaim the truth as he sees it. In the pursuit of the duties of his office, the minister may from time to time be under the necessity of giving expression to views at variance with the views of some, or even many, members of his congregation."[26] It seems to me that the prophetic chaplain must agree with Rabbi Wise and follow his advice. But there's more.

Prophecy can be thought of as a public exposition of a theological position and of telling the truth publicly. Truth is sometimes elusive and not as clear as what we might hope it would be. One person's clarity may be another person's murkiness; one person's truth may be another person's grave error. And theology, being what it is, requires a stance of great humility. Former Archbishop of Canterbury George Carey spoke to a group of Princeton students in November 2003 and said he could find no theological or scriptural justification for same-gender sexual expression. But then he added, "I could be wrong." We *all* could be wrong, and that's why we have to preserve the community so that we can keep talking and keep hearing one another and eventually, together, arrive at the truth. The need for unity applies not only within a particular Christian denomination, but across denominational boundaries, for the work of the Holy Spirit requires our full participation, with all points of view fully engaged.

The idea that we all could be wrong must not paralyze us. Instead it must cause us to be cautious and, even more than cautious, to be honest with ourselves. When as ministers we speak out against a perceived wrong, are we preaching from the gospel and from Christian tradition, or are we simply buying into the dominant culture? That is to say, is our prophecy the product of prayerful reflection and study, or is it something more self-serving or idiosyncratic? This, too, is the hard work of theology which informs prophecy — a self-examination about motives, possibly unexamined political beliefs, a desire to be accepted by those with whom we feel some affinity (Democrats or Republicans, Tories or Labour).

And so we take care in discerning what we will be prophetic about so that we do not confuse prophecy with politics. Theologian Ellen Charry speaks of sin as immaturity. The spiritually immature person is unable to obey the commandments to love God and to love neighbor.[27] Much of what passes for prophecy is really a manifestation of one's own political views and, thus, of one's spiritual immaturity. The Old Testament prophetic texts challenge us to move from the texts themselves to the particular circumstances of the current reality of injustice at the local or global levels and to find ways to be truly effective rather than to only posture. A true prophet, far from posturing, helps people mature in their relationship with God and in their treatment of others not only by calling people to a certain set of actions, but also by helping people discern exactly what God's will is with regard to the treatment of others under certain circumstances (e.g., war, abortion, homosexuality, poverty, the death penalty, and so on). An example of this is Archbishop Desmond Tutu's witness against apartheid in South Africa, and more recently against the United States' preemptive war on Iraq. Tutu's own charisma and spiritual maturity allow him to speak truth to power without a trace of posturing. Instead, his power and effectiveness as a prophet emanate directly from a clear and open proclamation of the gospel together with a centeredness and humility that can only come from a faithful prayer life.

What sometimes passes for prophetic ministry can be a deep and abiding anger that is expressed in unhelpful ways in the language of prophecy but only succeeds in polarizing people. Here again, Tutu's prophetic ministry that conveys an equal regard and love for the oppressors as well as the oppressed is an example of how outrage and anger are not necessarily the same thing.

One way of dealing with this dilemma is to find ways to raise hard questions in a way that forces everyone to look at them from all angles. Where divisive issues are concerned we tend quickly to become politicized and choose sides and then to talk only among ourselves. We create an echo chamber rather than a dialogue informed by and rooted in Christian love. What is the use of a prophecy that is preaching to the choir? Increased smugness? Further alienation of those who disagree? A chaplain as prophet can preach a gospel of peace and justice and still be open to differing sensibilities about how to arrive at peace and justice. And a chaplain as prophet can also allow for the reality that some would hold faithfulness to traditionalist views as at least as equally desirable as peace and justice. If the chaplain can succeed in doing both, then perhaps God's kingdom can be advanced while still preserving the community. Such a chaplain has achieved the objective of a true prophet — helping people know and love God and love their neighbors.

As an example of this approach I return to Archbishop Williams's comment about participating in an antiwar march (see p. 30 above). The core issue for him is the full and honest examination of one's position. There is Augustinian and Thomistic just war theory to consider as well as the ancient tradition of Christian pacifism that continues in the peace churches. And there are also strains of Christian tradition that one could argue would support an intervention such as was undertaken in Iraq in 2003 (though not very persuasively, in my opinion). Rather than to declare what the *right* position is, perhaps the chaplain's duty could be construed as creating opportunities for the issues to be debated openly and honestly, opportunities that will assure that all strains of scripture, tradition, and reason are employed in the enterprise, opportunities that enable all students to both arrive at a sound moral judgment on the issue and also learn from this experience how the process of arriving at a Christian moral judgment works in general.

For this to be successful the chaplain establishes rules for the debate. The chaplain makes available documents, Web sites, and other resources that offer students information on both sides of a question. And yet it is appropriate for the chaplain to limit the resources offered to students in the interest of civil discourse. For example, I have been on the alert for good Web sites that offer a reasoned and responsible traditionalist view concerning the human sexuality issues that divide the church. I was recently pleased to see an advertisement in a church magazine for a traditionalist Web site and immediately went to have a look. The first thing that caught my eye was a headline for a story about the Episcopal bishop of New Hampshire, V. Gene Robinson, that named him as "Vicky Gene Robinson." Now, it is true that this is, indeed, Bishop Robinson's full name. But it was clear from the context that the use of the name "Vicky," which Bishop Robinson himself does not use, was intended sarcastically. When I turned my attention to another Web site that purported to give a more progressive treatment of the issue, I was met with a headline that called a traditionalist bishop a "homophobe and a bigot." I linked neither of these Web sites to ours but continued the search. Calling each other "bigot" and "reactionary" and "apostate" short-circuits the process of discerning God's will.

Thus, a chaplain can be prophetic by creating an environment where dialogue can take place, where proponents of both sides of an issue feel respected and heard. The chaplain assures that there is no name calling and reminds everyone to choose his or her words carefully. Christian charity insists that we characterize the position of those with whom we disagree with accuracy and integrity by modeling such behavior ourselves. So, for example, we repeat reflectively the views of others and thus create an environment in which differing views can be heard and held in tension with respect.

Being prophetic means telling the truth, witnessing to God's love for all of creation, and giving hope to the hopeless. Thus, it is not difficult to find noncontroversial issues (at least within a body of Christian believers) about which to speak out. The chaplain as prophet can focus on these as a way, not only of being a Christian witness, but also to teach students how to respond to injustices. For example, most of my chaplain colleagues at Princeton and I participate in an annual event called "Gay Jeans Day." We wear jeans and give short speeches in support of the LGBT community. We join with the LGBT community and their supporters to show our concern for them and to decry attitudes and practices that are hurtful to them. Within the group of chaplains who participate there is a range of views on whether homosexuality is sinful and on such issues as gay marriage. But there is unanimity of the issue of love and respect for LGBT persons.

This example highlights that in drifting toward secular political issues we can often run the risk of sidestepping issues that are closer to home but more painful to confront. It is perhaps easier to join a peace march than it is to speak out against the ways that humans are degraded on campus by homophobia, alcohol and drug abuse, or by sexual exploitation. It is perhaps easier to speak out against poverty in Africa than it is to walk two blocks from campus to a poor neighborhood where college students could provide desperately needed tutoring for children. Here the chaplain as prophet has a wonderful opportunity to help students question their impulses that impel them to action or inaction. Are they politically or selfishly motivated, or are they motivated by a deep desire to serve the body of Christ and to be Christ-like?

In the classical Christian spiritual tradition, love of God and the desire to know God results in love of neighbor. As we come closer to God we simultaneously become more aware of, and sensitive to, the needs of others. But sometimes preaching that seeks to be prophetic has this order reversed and removes God from the equation; it decries injustice without making the Christian connection between love of God and love of neighbor. Such efforts may end up being partisan politics or amateur social work in the guise of Christian prophecy. The real power of genuine Christian prophecy stems from the centrality of God in our lives, which will make clear the path toward actions that best serve our neighbors, whether they are across the globe or across the dormitory hall.

A final word is in order regarding the timeliness of prophecy and campus ministry. The poor are always with us, Jesus said, and prophetic ministries concerning justice for the poor are never out of fashion. But on many campuses prophetic ministers made their early careers on being prophetic, often focusing on a particular evil or injustice such as the Vietnam War or, later, the oppression in Central America. In their time many of these prophetic ministries were a powerful witness to Christ's message of love and the biblical mandate of peace and justice for all. The trouble was that the world changed and some of these ministries did not. So dedicated were some of these prophetic ministers to their message that they had difficulty finding a new, more timely message when the circumstances that prompted their original call to prophecy changed — the Vietnam War ended, sanctuaries for political refugees from Central America were no longer so urgently needed. Yet some of these campus ministries continued to focus on these issues as if they were still as current as they had once been. More often than not, the chaplains involved were so engaged with maintaining their prophetic ministries that other necessary functions of the chaplaincy — pastoral care, stewardship, and so on — were sadly neglected, and the vibrancy of the ministry diminished over time.

In these instances it was as if Isaiah and Jeremiah were still warning Israel of impending doom in the early postexilic period. It's not that admonitions to be faithful were totally irrelevant; it's just that they were not quite as relevant as they once were. Prophetic messages must be timely and relevant to current circumstances and, equally important, must not dominate the life of the campus ministry to the point where its other functions are subordinated to extinction.

Paul exhorts us "not [to] be conformed to this world, but [to] be transformed by the renewing of [our] minds, so that [we] may discern what is the will of God — what is good and acceptable and perfect" (Rom. 12:2). Let us put hands and feet to our prayers!

# Chapter 5

# The Chaplain as Steward

*One who manages the affairs of an estate on behalf of
an employer; an administrator; one appointed
to manage the financial affairs of a congregation.*

———— ✠ ————

F OR CHRISTIANS who take seriously Jesus' command to love one
another as we love ourselves, the classic paradigm of a market
economy which speaks of scarcity and of winners and losers is deeply
disturbing. But economists have recently been pointing out that all
economic situations need not result in zero-sum outcomes like a game
of poker (i.e., where there must be a winner and a loser). They suggest
that in some games, like the game of Monopoly, cooperation between
two or more parties can lead to both parties being winners. Yet even
here, when this idea is applied to an entire economic system, there is
a limit to what each party can achieve, given that people in general
wish to maximize their own gain with little real concern for what
that may cost someone else, especially if that "someone else" lives
in a faraway place. And appetites for more are often insatiable —
"So they ate and were well filled, for he gave them what they craved.
But they did not stop their craving, though the food was still in their
mouths."[28]

An economy marked by scarcity and competition is a far cry from
God's economy. In Exodus 16:12 God rains down bread from heaven
on the wandering Israelites and then gives them fresh quail: "At twi-
light you shall eat meat, and in the morning you shall have your fill
of bread; then you shall know that I am the LORD your God." In

the next chapter they are given flowing water from a rock to quench their thirst. God's economy is one of abundance.

This understanding of God's abundant provision changes entirely how we think about our resources — and particularly our conversations about money. And since money is just a proxy for things of real value like time and tangible resources (buildings, books, information, and so on), our attitudes about this subject relate to how we marshal and care for everything that is needed in order to do campus ministry. The irony is that our discomfort with the entire subject can cause us to think more in terms of scarcity than abundance and to be poor stewards of what we have. Or maybe it is a faulty understanding of how we are to relate to God's abundance.

There is a story about a wealthy alumnus of a prestigious American university who for over twenty years donated fifteen thousand dollars annually to support a denominational campus ministry. When he died he gave over $50 million to the university but not one penny to the campus ministry. If we could ask him why he made no provisions in his will for the chaplaincy I suspect the answer would be, "They never asked me."

The effective chaplain as steward will strive to see how his or her attitudes about money — as well as about other resources — are part of being a good steward. One critically important resource is lay leadership, and so we begin our discussion of stewardship by thinking about the ministry's governing body and about its student leadership.

## The Governing Body

Like all ministry, being a steward is not a solo act. The campus ministry ideally has a broad base of support that is independent of the chaplain and that does not depend upon the chaplain for its life and continuity. Involving others begins with a governing body of lay and ordained people — including student representatives — who have the legal authority for the funds and the property owned by the ministry and who are responsible for overseeing the ministry to ensure that it is faithful to its stated mission. The organization's bylaws and articles of incorporation will dictate how many board members will constitute the governing body, how they will be elected, and how long they will serve. The bylaws will also spell out the duties of the entire board as well as the duties of officers such as the chair, the secretary, and the treasurer, and how often the board will meet.

It may seem more expedient for the chaplain to lead the governing board, especially if the members of the board lack the interest and the energy to govern. And it is simply easier to do things on one's own and in one's own way without interference, so some chaplains eventually might well use Frank Sinatra's signature song — "I did it my way" — as their own.

The danger here is that the ministry can, and often does, swiftly depart from its originally intended core mission and can begin to use resources unwisely. A common manifestation of this is the chaplaincy that, although its charter specifies that it will primarily serve undergraduates, has become focused on a particular segment of the university's life such as a ministry to the faculty and staff, or a ministry concerned with medical ethics centered at the medical school. A more serious and, alas, all too common problem is that a weak or uninvolved governing body can result in a chaplain who has retired on the job. In other instances, a passive governing board will not notice, or if they do notice not react, when the focus of a campus ministry has become stuck in the past in ways I alluded to at the end of the chapter on the chaplain as prophet.

For example, during the Reagan administration a large urban state university chaplaincy declared itself a sanctuary for Central Americans caught up in the political turmoil of that time. Many students were involved, and the sanctuary initiative was the central focus of a vibrant prophetic ministry. Twenty years later, while there still may be a need for a public sanctuary, this ministry has virtually no undergraduate student involvement, and no one can remember the last time a Central American came to campus seeking sanctuary. Yet the sanctuary remains the most prominent feature of this ministry.

Because of such issues, it is in the chaplain's and the ministry's best interests that a governing body govern itself and not be controlled by the chaplain. A strong, independent governing board is much more useful to the chaplain than a passive one at times of controversy or fund-raising, for example. An active and involved board helps the chaplain control and account for revenues and expenditures, with a treasurer disbursing all but the chaplain's discretionary funds so as to guard against any charge of misuse of funds. The board also can be useful in supporting the chaplain emotionally and spiritually and in being an advocate for the ministry with external funding sources, faculty, staff, administrators, and alumni. A chaplain with a strong governing body is rarely alone and far out on a limb when there are difficult issues to face, such as, for example, threatened budget cuts from outside funding sources. A well-functioning governing board frees up the chaplain to concentrate on those other functions of ministry covered in other chapters and absolves the chaplain from direct involvement in matters that will be distractions from ministry.

## Student Leadership

Whereas the governing body represents the formal organizational structure of the ministry, the student leadership represents its life-blood. With a motto of "Let students do it!" the chaplain harnesses a rich resource of creativity and energy. Moreover, students nearly always have their ears closer to the ground when it comes to being aware of campus trends and relating to their peers. Student leaders will also be able to advise a chaplain whether a new idea or initiative is workable and worth pursuing or whether a different tack should be taken. As in any local church setting, an idea flourishes when it captures the energy of the congregation, and should typically be dropped if it doesn't.

A few years ago a graduate student began making communion bread for our weekly worship. Everyone enjoyed the texture and the taste of this bread, and it was a wonderful addition to our overall worship experience. When she got her degree and left the university, several students asked why we were using store-bought bread instead of the homemade bread, with the implicit expectation that I or my wife would take over making the bread. When I invited them to make the bread they demurred, thus demonstrating that this was not their highest priority.

Students are not only a valuable asset for the present; they are an asset critical to the church's future. Thus, part of the chaplain's job as a steward is not only to use these assets for the current needs of the ministry, but also to invest them wisely for the future of the church. In this way leaders for the church are raised up and prepared for future leadership roles in the wider church. On my first day on the job I met a young man who had just been confirmed in the Episcopal Church the previous spring during his first year at college. Chris was not very involved in the ministry, but over the year I was able to draw him in; he soon assumed a major leadership role beginning in his third year at the university. By the time he graduated he was thinking of ordained ministry, and nearly four years to the day after I met him Chris began seminary.

An investment in the development of future leaders of the church that would have immediate benefits for the ministry would be to work with students to build a student-led and student-run leadership group called, for example, the "cabinet" or "leadership team" or "board" with two or three "conveners" or "chairs" or "officers" or "wardens." The name of the student group and the titles of its leaders might be formal ones like those just mentioned, or they might be more whimsical (one campus ministry calls its student leadership group "The Dream Team"). But whatever they are called it is always best to empower the student leaders with *real* decision-making authority, and they must be given the full responsibility to implement programs. The chaplain who is an effective steward of students' talents and gifts will resist the temptation to rescue the ministry from students who do not meet obligations that have been agreed upon by doing the work for them. For example, a weekly dinner event requires planning, shopping for food, preparing and serving the meal, and cleanup. When students become busy with other obligations and do not attend to the requirements of the weekly dinner, it is usually best for the chaplain not to step in and do the work. The occasional times when there is no food or when students must be drafted to clean up the kitchen will send the message that students are in charge of the dinner. Such crises also beg the question of what kind of weekly program the students really desire as opposed to following practices of the past or the chaplain's agenda.

Students can be enlisted for leadership roles early in their college careers and progress to more significant roles as they continue to show interest in being part of the ministry. A student who is put in charge of greeting newcomers to worship services one year may be willing and able to take on other roles later on. Peer ministry, discussed in chapter 1, and the role of "chaplain's assistant" are other ways to involve students in the leadership of the ministry in a way that makes use of all their talents and gifts. Students can be the "eyes and ears" of the ministry and thus extend the reach of the chaplain. People who are leaders are, of course, one of the ministry's most valuable resources. So are the facilities and locations where ministry can occur on the campus.

## Facilities and Location

The real estate dictum about location, location, location is true also with regard to a campus ministry's facilities, but the type of facility is important too. Princeton is usually thought of as a Presbyterian university (although formal ties to the Presbyterian Church have long since been cut) and that church had a lively campus ministry in the first half of the twentieth century, based as it was in a wonderful Victorian-style house across the street from the campus, very near the house owned by the Episcopal Church at Princeton. As mentioned in the introduction, the Presbyterians sold their house in the 1950s with a view toward basing their ministry in a church that is actually on the campus. A half-century later the Presbyterian ministry has less than half the number of students involved in weekly services and activities than the Episcopal Church does. They have had wonderful, gifted chaplains, and the main difference between the two ministries lies in the different facilities available to each of them. The Episcopal presence on campus is homey whereas the Presbyterian presence is churchy. In a similar vein, the Roman Catholic chaplain at Rutgers University in New Brunswick, New Jersey, told of renovating an old church building near the main campus saying, "You can fix a bad building, but you can't fix a bad location."

Adam Kittrell makes a distinction between "campus ministry" and "ministry to the campus."[29] Kittrell calls ministry to the campus a ministry carried out by a local church and sees this as a different type of ministry from that carried out by a person whose *sole* responsibility is to the campus. He might have added that the distinction holds with regard to the type of facility employed by the ministry as well as the people involved, as the Princeton experience shows.

The "dream scenario" for a campus ministry is to have both a homey building where the chaplain lives and where students can gather for informal worship and fellowship, relaxation, and meals, *and* a churchy building for more formal worship services. The closer the homey building is to the "caravan routes" of the campus, the better. I was recently surprised to learn that Procter House at Princeton — the home of the Episcopal Church at Princeton — is considered to be "off campus" even though it is surrounded on all sides by university-owned buildings and is a five-minute walk from the center of campus. It's also ideal if the building has a welcoming and informative sign and looks homey rather than institutional. And some sort of kitchen facility is a necessity! A university chapel that is owned and maintained by the university and that allows any religious group to schedule regular and special services is the perfect complement.

As discussed in chapters 1 and 6, signs and banners and other welcoming and informative devices that draw students into the space are critically important to "getting the people into the tent."

Many campus ministries and churches have assets that are not being used to their fullest advantage for the ministry. Underused buildings and land present opportunities to be creative and entrepreneurial stewards. An excellent example comes from the University of Minnesota in Minneapolis where the Episcopal campus ministry had a chapel set on a fifteen-thousand-square-foot lot adjacent to the campus. The chapel had been built in the 1960s for a few hundred worshipers but never had more than a few dozen on a typical Sunday. There were other inefficiencies inherent in the building, and it was a drain on financial resources to keep it in good repair and to heat it during those long, cold Minnesota winters.

The chaplaincy entered into a partnership with a real estate developer, which built a new building that houses the chaplain's office as well as a smaller chapel. The building also has apartments, including one floor dedicated to housing university students who elect to join an "intentional community." The church continues to own the land, and the real estate developer owns the building for a sixty-year period, at which time the building reverts to the church.

Whatever the circumstances are regarding buildings and facilities, the chaplain as steward will be diligent in assuring that the building maintenance is kept current. A chaplain who is not familiar or comfortable with issues surrounding building maintenance will want to recruit knowledgeable help from governing board members and other volunteers. By annually earmarking funds for preventive maintenance, facilities can be kept in good repair. Deferred maintenance is no maintenance, and eventually a neglected building will cost more than ongoing upkeep ever would have.

While facilities are the most tangible and visible resources a ministry can have, a good steward will pay attention to a less tangible resource, but no less important one — namely, information.

## Information

Recently a new chaplain arrived at a large state university where, she had been told, there was an active cadre of students and a solid history of annual fund-raising from alumni. When she arrived on the scene, however, there were almost no students involved, and she was unable to locate lists of students. Similarly, there were only slivers of information about alumni. Not much to go on for a new chaplain! Happily, she was resourceful and creative and was able to build up a list of students and alumni that, although small at the beginning, allowed her to get the ministry reenergized. In the case of alumni the chaplain will wish to maintain a list not only of those who were involved with the ministry while they were at college, but also of those who have become active in the church since graduation. The latter will be identified in a more or less haphazard and serendipitous fashion as the chaplain meets and greets alumni and friends of alumni and sometimes even friends of friends of relatives of alumni! We have been very successful in identifying alumni who are active in our church with a simple advertising campaign. One ad was placed in Princeton's alumni magazine, which is read thoroughly by alumni. The ad said "Episcopalian? Please tell us!" and included the name of the ministry and contact information. Then we placed an ad in two major church publications that are widely read by Episcopalians. These ads read, "Did you go to Princeton? Please tell us!" These ads generated dozens of new contacts we would never have known of otherwise.

Every opportunity to identify a potential friend of the ministry can be seized, and the information can be stored in a coherent and safe way for future use by oneself and one's successors. Look in all the file cabinets and desk drawers at your chaplaincy for any information on past students or alumni who have been involved, then look up their current addresses in the university alumni directory if you have one. You can also ask pastors and lay leaders in parishes to send you names and addresses of their parishioners who are alumni of your university (you could even ask the head of your church's judicatory to send out the request for you). We tried this in the Diocese of New Jersey by asking those attending our annual convention to fill out a form telling us where they went to college. We then shared these contacts — there were over one hundred! — with all the chaplains in the diocese.

Ideally, the university will maintain this information for the ministry simply by coding the computerized alumni file for religious affiliation. This assures that the alumni file is updated as people change their addresses and telephone numbers. However, the ministry will still need to maintain its own list locally to keep track of gifts and donations. The university, even if willing to share alumni address information with each campus ministry, is unlikely to maintain gift records for each ministry. As we discuss below, these gift records are essential to a successful annual and capital gift campaign.

## Endowment Management

Every campus ministry will want to develop an endowment to assist with its current operating expenses and to assure its future viability.[30] Some already have endowments, but those that do not would do well to build one. Those with endowments will periodically wish to examine whether they need to grow in order to account for slippage in investments over time and to expand the ministry. Ministries that receive funds from a regional or national church body that cover all annual operating expenses would be very prudent to consider seriously building an endowment "while the sun is shining" against the eventuality — and very real possibility — that the funding body's budget priorities may shift and leave campus ministries with reduced funding or none at all. A robust endowment assures independence from other bodies and a secure future. We examine how to develop the endowment when we discuss fund-raising below, after we first examine how to maintain an endowment.

An endowment is a fund set aside for a particular purpose that is invested so that it will produce income for its own growth over the years as well as for current operating expenses. Thus, the endowment is best invested in a manner that maximizes its growth *and* its long-term security. These two goals are in tension as a completely secure fund (such as a simple interest-bearing bank account) will not grow very much. On the other hand, a fund that is designed only to maximize growth without regard to the risk involved will likely suffer large losses which may offset any large gains that may be achieved (e.g., a fund that is invested solely in high-technology stocks). It would be as imprudent to keep the entire fund squirreled away in a bank account where it would never grow as it would be to risk it all on high-risk stocks.

It is best to have the endowment managed by a firm that specializes in church or other not-for-profit organization funds. This will mean that fees must be paid, and it is important to assure that the fund is managed by a firm that charges fees based only on the size of the endowment rather than charging a fee each time a stock or bond is bought or sold. The former fee arrangement gives the fund manager an incentive to manage the endowment prudently, whereas the latter arrangement rewards the manager for "churning" the holdings of the endowment in order to generate transaction fees, but may also lower the value of the fund. The chaplaincy will be wise to avoid the understandable temptation to have a member of the church or member of the governing body who happens to be a professional fund manager handle the endowment. This can lead to awkwardness when things do not go well. Even worse is having a friend of the chaplaincy who has no professional expertise manage the fund on a pro bono basis. It is all very well for an amateur investor to manage his or her own money, but it is not the best stewardship for an endowment for a church ministry to be managed by an amateur.

A professional fund advisor will suggest the best mix of stocks (high- to moderate-risk investments), bonds (low-risk investments), and cash (no risk) that the endowment should be invested in. The mix will depend upon the objectives of the fund, and the objectives will depend upon how large the fund is compared with the necessary "draw" on the fund for annual operating expenses and other factors; the fund manager should be able to explain these items clearly to a chaplain and board members who have no prior experience or knowledge concerning financial management.

Endowment funds may be restricted or unrestricted. Restricted funds legally may only be used for designated purposes. For example, a fund may be designated for programs only, but not for salaries or for building maintenance. A supporter of your ministry may wish to establish a restricted endowment fund that pays for the ministry's weekly fellowship dinners or for an annual series of guest speakers. Unrestricted funds, on the other hand, may be used for any purpose within the scope of the organization, and the purpose is determined by the governing board. When there is more than one fund owned by a chaplaincy, the chaplain will want to be very clear about whether each fund is restricted or unrestricted and, if restricted, for what purposes the fund may be used.

The amount of money that is taken out of an endowment on an annual basis is critically important to its long-term survival. When endowments are reasonably large, say in excess of five hundred thousand dollars, there is a tendency to miss the long-term consequences of taking too much money out. Income from an endowment of this size or greater could easily be at the level of the chaplain's salary as well as other important budget items. A good rule of thumb is to keep annual spending at or below 4.5 percent of the average size of the entire endowment for the previous three years. A draw greater than that will diminish the endowment owing to fluctuations in market performance and inflation and eventually lead to its total demise — a demise that actually accelerates over time. Since this is such a common problem with church endowments, let's pause to consider two different scenarios with the same starting point in terms of endowment size. Those of you who are "not numbers people" are urged to take a deep breath and force yourself to follow along. You'll soon see that this is not really all that complicated.

Let's begin by assuming that there are two endowments, each with five hundred thousand dollars in assets at a given point in time and that their growth rate over a long time range (ten years or more) will average 7.5 percent per year. At this given point of time let us further assume that the draw on the first endowment is forty thousand dollars, or 8.0 percent of the total, and that it will keep up with inflation by an annual increase of 3 percent. Finally, let's assume that the draw on the second endowment is twenty-two thousand dollars or 4.5 percent of the total with the same annual growth rate of 3 percent to cover inflation.

The two graphs on the following page tell the story for each endowment, one rather grim and the other quite bright. The first endowment's spending rate thirteen years out from the beginning has grown geometrically to 19 percent, and one can see that by the third year the total holdings already are in decline. The critical point to grasp here is that by about the eighth year the decline has accelerated to a point of virtually no return. That is to say, unless the draw on the endowment is cut almost to nothing, the endowment will be completely depleted in just a few more years after the time period shown on this graph.

The second graph shows a healthy growth in the size of the endowment at a draw rate of 4.5 percent. One might reasonably ask why one could not draw at a slightly higher rate, say 5.0 percent, since it appears the top line is growing so well. The answer is that increasing the draw even slightly above 4.5 percent, and sustaining it at that level, will retard the endowment's overall growth, perhaps imperceptibly at first, but eventually to a dangerous level. Drawing upon an endowment at a rate higher than 4.5 percent per year is like taking a narcotic drug. It feels good at first and even seems to be good for you. But in the end it will probably kill you. In theological terms, it is just simply poor stewardship.

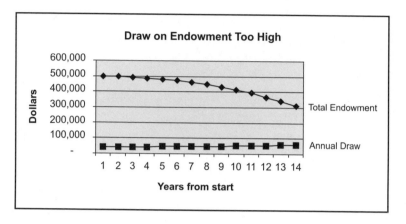

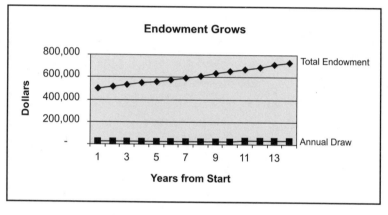

When church organizations get into a situation where such a precipitous decline in an endowment occurs, one often hears someone, usually a clergy person, say, "I'm just not good with numbers." This is an unacceptable excuse, one worthy of the "wicked and slothful" servant in the parable of the talents in Matthew 25. The chaplain as steward will rise above any hesitations he or she may have about handling money and accept the responsibility at least to ask such simple and straightforward questions of experts as "Are we spending too much of the endowment?" and, "What will happen over a twenty-year period if we keep spending the endowment as we are now?" Of course no one, the chaplain least of all, may really want to know the answer to these tough questions if the answer means that changes in program or even in the employment of the chaplain will have to be made, but they are nonetheless necessary to ask on at least an annual basis.

A final word concerning the discipline required to manage an endowment relates to spending during times of rapid market growth such as those experienced during the economic boom of the 1990s. During such times when the endowment is growing at a double-digit rate, it is tempting to increase the draw above the 4.5 percent level with the justification that the rapid growth of the market allows for a temporary increase in spending. There are two serious flaws in this practice. One is that once a spending level has been increased it is extremely difficult to return to the lower level of spending. No one wants to face the pain of making cuts in the budget. The second, more serious flaw is that the graphs shown above are based on assumptions about *average* market growth (7.5 percent per year) and inflation (3.0 percent per year). An average takes into consideration the temporary peaks as well as the temporary valleys in the performance of the financial markets. Many organizations with endowments forgot this age-old rule of market averages and now regret having increased their spending in the quixotic expectation that the heady performance of the 1990s would last indefinitely. It did not! Put another way, if you want to increase your spending during a booming market, you also have to be willing to cut your spending when the boom times are over, as they surely one day will be.

## Fund-Raising

In the previous section we discussed endowments. Many campus ministries do not have endowments, and fund-raising thus becomes essential. But even those few ministries with large endowments are wise to have an annual fund drive and periodic capital campaigns in order to assure that the ministry's wider community of friends and alumni are spiritually and emotionally invested in its well-being.

Also, as mentioned earlier, endowments are usually in need of a periodic "boost" of new funds to keep in line with increasing program demands, market disappointments, and higher costs.

Before a ministry even begins to ask for money, it is essential that it first do something worthwhile — a ministry to young people rooted in the good news of Jesus Christ. Then tell others about it! As the ministry begins to develop a record of service to the university, the chaplain and the governing body can identify people who believe in the work you are doing and get them engaged in the life of the ministry. Once this is done, these friends of the ministry can be asked to support it. And when they do, they are thanked effusively, and more than once. Our ministry was recently given funds to purchase new furniture for our common room. In addition to the standard thank-you letter from me, the donor received two handwritten notes from students who liked the new furniture so much they wanted to thank him personally. He was so pleased to receive these notes he called me to tell me and at the end of the conversation asked, "Is there anything I can do to help you?" He never mentioned the letter I sent him! The best motivation for giving is a good experience of giving. Let's unpack these concepts a bit more by examining *three foundations* for fund-raising and *three types* of fund-raising.[31]

The first foundation is *structure*, aspects of which we have already discussed above. A governing body must be in place, and the ministry must have some official legal status either as part of a larger organization (e.g., a church parish) or on its own. In the United States a not-for-profit organization is designated as a 501(c)3 organization under the federal tax code. There are similar "registered charity" organizational designations in the United Kingdom and other countries.[32] These organizations can receive gifts from donors, who in turn receive a tax deduction for the gift. There are annual reporting requirements for these organizations in the United States, United Kingdom, and other countries. Check with an attorney to be sure your organization is in compliance. In addition to whatever bylaws the government will require for the organization, the chaplaincy should have a set of policies that spell out in detail its investment policies, spending policies (e.g., no more than 4.5 percent of endowment per year), budgeting process, and policies for handling various kinds of gifts such as stocks, life insurance, and property. Another piece of the structure of fund-raising is the donor database, which we have already discussed. Be relentless in finding names to add to your list, and keep the list strictly confidential! Finally, the structure of fund-raising involves an annual schedule of events such as newsletter production and the timing of the annual appeal.

*Awareness* is the second foundation of fund-raising, and this subject receives a more complete treatment in the chapter on chaplain as herald. No one will give money or assets to your chaplaincy unless you first tell your story — what you are doing, what impact it is having, why it is important, how your ministry fits in with the wider life of the university and the church, and so on. Thus, it is important to communicate what you're doing at least once a year, and quarterly is even better. Also, publicize your desire to have your ministry named in wills and estate plans (legacy society). The chief reason people do not name campus ministries in their wills is that nobody ever asks them to! If you don't have a Web site, develop one as soon as you can. Seize every opportunity you can find to trumpet your ministry's accomplishments to your alumni; they will love you for it!

*Response* is the third foundation of a fund-raising effort. The chaplain must nurture relationships. For example, the best response to an inquiry about your ministry is a personal visit, or if that is not possible, a telephone call. Donors who give year after year, even small amounts, should also be called and thanked. In order to be able to do this, gifts must be tracked over time. Every giver should be thanked more than once and in different ways — letters, handwritten notes, telephone calls. Finally, you should publish your donor list in your newsletter.

Now we examine briefly the three types of fund-raising. Perhaps the most familiar is *ordinary giving*. This is the annual campaign in

which people on the chaplaincy's mailing list are asked for a donation to help defray annual operating costs. We spoke a moment ago
about regular communications from the chaplain to everyone on the
chaplaincy's mailing list in the form of a newsletter at least on an annual basis, and preferably on a quarterly basis. Each of these mailings
should include an envelope in which a potential donor can send in
a check. At least once a year there should be included in these mailings an explicit, direct appeal for donations. Each donor should be
thanked, and the donations should be recorded in the name database.
By keeping track of where the donations are coming from, you can
encourage those who have given in past years, but not the current
year, to give again. At the end of each year a report can be run from
the database showing the names and addresses of those donors who
gave a gift in the previous year but not in the current year (in fund-
raising circles this is called a LYBUNT report for "Last Year but Not
This"). Then a letter can be sent to each person on the report showing what they gave last year and asking them to give again. Good
examples of LYBUNT letters can be found through a search of the
Internet and adapted as needed. The first LYBUNT letter our ministry
ever sent out netted over three thousand dollars in four weeks!

The next type of fund-raising is *extraordinary giving,* which is
based on an occasional effort, perhaps every five or ten years. The
capital campaign is an appeal for major gifts with a specific purpose
(building a building, creating or supplementing an endowment, and
the like) and a specific goal. Major gifts require a major effort, and it
is usually wise to hire a consultant to help with a capital campaign,
which may last for a few years. Most chaplains and board members
have little or no experience with capital campaigns, so it is best to
engage consultants who have experience with churches and campus
ministries and who have sound, verifiable reputations. These consultants should always be paid hourly or daily fees, not a percentage of
the money raised. This will assure that you will get sound advice in
keeping with your Christian mission. A good consultant will coach
the chaplain and the governing body through various phases and

steps of a capital campaign. The following is an excellent example of a description of these phases, used with permission from the Web site of Holliman Associates in Newport, Pennsylvania.[33]

◆ ◆ ◆

## Discernment Services

◆ Not all organizations are ready for a capital campaign. Ideas must be articulated and fully communicated with a constituency. Visions are modified as input is received.

◆ The hard-worn experience of many campaigns enables Holliman Associates to accurately assess the level of support that exists for your project and how well you have articulated and communicated your proposed plans.

◆ Often, a precampaign discernment phase is required. By means of group facilitation, newsletters, small group meetings, and other materials and events, your vision is shared and refined.

◆ The process builds relationships and rallies a spirit of common purpose among your membership, well before the campaign begins.

◆ Discernment begins to capture the hearts and imaginations of your people, ensuring their enthusiastic and generous involvement throughout a subsequent campaign.

## Feasibility Studies

After a period of discernment, the next step is the feasibility study.

◆ Critical decisions about the scope and projects of the campaign, who should lead the campaign, when it should begin, and what the goal should be need to be made in the context of current, unbiased, and accurate information.

◆ A well-designed feasibility study provides that information. It also sparks interest in the proposed campaign and establishes credibility.

- ◆ In general, the feasibility study:

  - analyzes levels of understanding and support
  - identifies major donors
  - validates the case statement
  - defines the campaign time frame
  - ascertains the amount of money that can be raised to advance your ministry and service

- ◆ In addition, the study gives constituents an opportunity to share in the vision, to offer their own ideas, and to take further ownership of the campaign. It also suggests the extent of the activities and the length of time needed for continued communications.

## Capital Campaigns

- ◆ Once you decide to launch a capital campaign, strong leadership and organization become crucial.

- ◆ Drawing upon years of experience, Holliman Associates provides proven campaign strategies that complement your culture and leadership style. Each campaign is personalized to fit your unique circumstances, drawing upon your strengths, calling upon the right people at the right times, focusing your effort to maximize the time and effectiveness of your volunteers.

- ◆ Some church and charity campaigns require full-time on-site service. Others need only periodic in-and-out guidance. This flexible approach results in the efficient use of our skills and the good stewardship of your resources.

- ◆ In addition to solid, on-site guidance, Holliman Associates offers user-friendly campaign management software to help you keep your effort on track.

- ◆ The customizable Holliman Campaign Manager program...

  - coordinates and tracks worker solicitation activity
  - produces solicitation status

- reports and records gifts and pledges
- produces acknowledgments, mailing labels, reminder notices, tax receipts, and financial reports — including pledge income projections

◆ In the end, strong management does more than help your campaign reach its goal. A winning campaign identifies and develops leadership, promotes positive awareness, recruits fresh talent, taps new resources, fosters a sense of ministry, builds up annual giving, and improves the channel of communication for years to come.  ◆ ◆ ◆

Finally, the third type of fund-raising is *ultimate giving.* In fund-raising circles this is called "planned giving." The most common type of planned giving is the will or bequest by which a person designates that all or part of his or her estate will be given to the chaplaincy upon his or her death. In most states and countries it is possible to add a codicil (i.e., an addendum to a preexisting will). In any case, there are various kinds of bequests, which the following examples are meant to illustrate:

1. *Specific bequest* is a donation of a particular amount of money (say, for example, fifty thousand dollars) or a particular piece of property (such as a valuable painting, jewelry, a house, or a plot of land). For example:

   I bequeath ten thousand dollars to the Episcopal Church at Princeton University.

2. *Residuary bequest* is a donation of all or part of the assets remaining in an estate after debts, expenses, and other specific bequests have been paid. For example:

   I give, bequeath, or devise 75 percent of the rest, residue, and remainder of the property, both real and personal, wherever situated, which I may own or be entitled to at my death, to the Episcopal Church at Princeton University.

3. *Contingent bequest* is a donation that takes effect only if the primary beneficiary or beneficiaries of the bequest predecease the person making the will. For example:

> If neither my husband nor any descendants of mine survive me, then I give, bequeath, and devise all the rest, residue, and remainder of the property, both real and personal, wherever situated which I may own or be entitled to at my death, to the Episcopal Church at Princeton University.

There are a wide variety of other gifts which can be made that will provide the donor with a current tax deduction and protect heirs from certain taxes. There are also instruments by which a person may make a gift of money to the chaplaincy that will provide to the donor a monthly income stream for the remainder of the donor's life with the principal amount reverting to the chaplaincy upon the donor's death. There are numerous resources on the Internet that explain various kinds of planned gifts. The key to getting them, however, is to ask. There are many stories told of elderly alumni who are active church members whose attorneys asked, "Why did you not name the chaplaincy at your university in your will?" who reply, "Because they never asked me." Remember the story told earlier about the loyal supporter who left his campus ministry out of his will! Getting planned gifts takes a great deal of patience, but the chaplain should always take the opportunity to mention wills and other planned gifts in any annual or capital appeal. The chaplain as steward should also work to identify attorneys and financial advisors who may be in a position to know people who would support your ministry. These professionals can be encouraged to keep your ministry in mind whenever they are approached by someone seeking advice about wills and estate plans.

No one I know ever went to seminary and entered the ministry wanting to maintain buildings and manage information and money. I certainly didn't! But our ministry depends on these resources to be successful and to thrive well beyond our tenures on the job. Attending to these admittedly unglamorous tasks is much easier and more rewarding when we remember that God calls us to be good stewards of all we have been given so abundantly and that it is actually an important part of our ministry to help others form a spiritually healthy relationship with what they have been given. Let's turn now to a discussion about how a campus ministry makes itself known to the campus and how it proclaims the gospel.

# Chapter 6

# The Chaplain as Herald

*A messenger or envoy; one who announces.*

—————— ✠ ——————

**T**HE WORD "HERALD" does not appear often in translations of the New Testament and, in some versions, such as the King James (Authorized Version), it is not used at all. The most interesting use of the word for our purposes is in the two letters to Timothy, where the sense of the word as it is defined in modern dictionaries is "to be a sign that something important, and often good, is starting to happen, or to make something publicly known, especially by celebrating or praising it.... "[34] In each of these letters the writer is giving instructions to the church based on the good news of Jesus Christ. As chaplains we speak equally to the whole congregation and to the particularity of individuals. We are God's ambassadors to the church on campus as a whole and to its constituent members, and we are thus called to be communicators.

The Greek word for "herald" in the New Testament is also translated as "preacher" in the King James Bible. This is an appropriate rendering, because as God's ambassadors we are called upon not only to give instruction but to proclaim the gospel and to celebrate it with great joy. For most students, faculty, and staff the chaplain's preaching will be the most frequent experience of the chaplain as herald and perhaps the most important. Indeed, for many it may be their only experience of the chaplain's ministry. And so, while this chapter is about the chaplain as a communicator in general, we begin with preaching.

## Preaching

Preaching anywhere, but especially in a university setting, is an opportunity to proclaim the gospel if the preacher can manage to avoid two major pitfalls: the temptation to make yourself the hero, or at least the major figure, of most of your sermons; and the temptation to be too clever. The best antidote for the first temptation is to be very intentional about making Jesus Christ the hero of every sermon. Students at a southwestern university complained that until recently they could not find a place on campus where the gospel was preached. When I asked them why, they told me that one chaplain can always be relied upon to tell a long-winded story about his dog, his kids, his wife, or himself in which he usually either saves the day or becomes aware of some particular personal failing but hardly ever mentions the day's scripture lessons. Another chaplain preaches sermons on a regular basis on social justice themes which feature her own heroic efforts to feed the hungry, clothe the naked, and heal the sick. Still another chaplain has a habit of inserting his favorite sports team into every sermon and asking for prayers for their victory in the next game. The students reported these unhappy tales in the process of telling me that a new chaplain had come to campus the previous term and had quickly developed a reputation of giving sermons that were wonderful examples of biblical exegesis, sound theology, and inspired social concern.

These students made two interesting points about the new chaplain's preaching. The first was that it was his faithfulness to the biblical texts and his attempts to impart a theological message that called their attention to exactly what had been so unsatisfying about the other sermons they had heard on campus. The other was that they said that the new chaplain was not the best speaker they had ever heard, nor was he riveting in any sense of the word. He was just an ordinary minister preaching an extraordinary message — one that was self-consciously not his own, but Jesus Christ's. Students are quite adept at spotting the self-celebratory professor, football coach,

roommate, and classmate. All the practice students get in spotting —
and disdaining — the self-celebration of others comes to bear when
they listen to sermons. A self-congratulatory sermon might be just
the thing to assure that visiting students will never return, whereas
a Christ-centered sermon holds the possibility that they will be so
intrigued by the differentness of such good news that they will want
to return again and again. As Peter Gomes suggests, "The preacher
and the listener must together enter into the text in order that the
text may enter into their hearts, their minds, and their world."[35]

Being clever is another problem. Cleverness is probably the most
highly prized quality in an academic setting, and some chaplains find
it irresistible to engage in the sport of being clever. Cleverness is
used by students to show off what they know, and faculty members
sometimes use clever remarks and creative and provocative turns of
phrase to assert intellectual dominance and, in more benign cases, to
stimulate interest in their topic or just to be amusing.

In the late 1940s a preacher in Princeton was preaching one Sunday
in August on the anniversary of the atomic bombings of Japan a few
years earlier. He went on at length about the evils of the bombings and
of the evil motives of those who developed the bomb. In doing so he
also misquoted a T. S. Eliot poem, which did not go unnoticed by many
in the congregation. After the service, as he greeted departing worshipers, some of whom corrected the misquotation, along came a navy
admiral in full dress uniform who introduced himself as having been
a member of the Manhattan Project that developed the bomb. While
the preacher was still reeling from this encounter a kindly looking
gentleman shook his hand and said, "Good morning. I'm T. S. Eliot."

People come to church to be edified and challenged spiritually, not
to be impressed by the preacher. Communal church worship offers
the unique opportunity of proclaiming the gospel with vigor. The
chaplain is called upon to do what a professor in the classroom cannot: point the way toward a deeper relationship with God through
Jesus Christ.[36] As a chaplain gains acceptance in the community, invitations will be forthcoming to participate in forums and other events

where the chaplain is expected to share a religious point of view related to the topic under discussion. This presents the chaplain with an opportunity, in perhaps a less obvious way, to proclaim the good news. Blessedly, some of the chaplains all over the United States, and the world, who were called upon in the hours and days after the terrorist attacks of September 11, 2001, to comment on the religious dimensions of the horror took the opportunity to speak appropriately and prophetically about the Christian imperative to love our enemies and to examine root causes for such evil acts, and to make the distinction between the culpable and the innocent.

A variation on preaching is to write letters to the editor or editorials for the university newspaper or magazine regarding topics of the day that call out for a religious, even prophetic, point of view. But there are other ways in which the chaplain functions as herald on the university campus, and many of these have to do with how the campus ministry communicates with its several constituencies.

## Web Sites and the Internet

University students are constantly using Internet search engines (Google and others like it) to find information, and there is even a common and popular practice of "googling" a person's name — a professor, a friend, and, yes, a chaplain! — to see what information about the person can be gleaned from the Internet. The Internet has become one of the primary sources of information on any topic for university students. Thus, it is essential that the campus ministry have an attractive, well-maintained Web site as an information portal to your ministry. Really good Web sites often had their origins in an effort simply to get the names, addresses, and times of worship and other activities up on the Web. This is a reasonable place to start and not that difficult to accomplish. From there Web sites can evolve into much more.

The best way to begin is to find a student who is familiar with Web page design and knows the ins and outs of getting a Web page up and running on a server. Often a college or university will support campus ministry Web sites. If that is not possible, other options can be explored, including getting help from local and national church organizations or vendors that sell professionally designed Web templates that can be adapted to local use. In some cases templates can be purchased for under one hundred dollars (see, for example, *www.netidnow.com*).

After you get a preliminary Web site up and running with basic information (your campus ministry: who, what, where, and when), begin work in collaboration with your student experts to make the Web site a more integral part of your ministry — a sort of "associate chaplain" who never sleeps. Thus, the content could have lots of detailed information about upcoming worship services and other events; what your worship is like; statements regarding the Christian faith and beliefs and practices; sermons that have been given in your chaplaincy, including those given by students and other guest preachers; spirituality and prayer information, including links to pages that have the entire forms for daily prayer online; links to other sites concerning your denomination, the Bible, and Christianity in general; and a page encouraging visitors to contribute financial resources to your ministry. The chaplain will want to maintain control over the content of the site and should ensure that its look and feel are appropriate. Students will be an endless source of creative ideas about how best to make the site attractive to other students and will usually be more technically proficient than the average clergyperson.

Once you have a Web site, it is important to include the Web address on *every* publication, poster, banner, or e-mail so as to direct as much traffic to the site as possible. This is especially critical if your Web site has a wide array of resources and links that will help seekers understand more about Christianity and what you have to offer students, faculty, and staff. That the site be well maintained with current, up-to-date information and that "stale" notices and information be removed periodically and in a timely fashion is therefore critical. Nothing will limit the use of your Web site more than a notice for an event that happened last year or even last semester. Such stale information can also suggest that your entire ministry is a bit lifeless.

Once you have done all this, submit the address to various search engines like Google. Make sure that key words that would easily be found by a search engine are in the text on the first page of your Web site. This step will assure that a search using a word that describes your religious affiliation and the name of your college or university will bring up your ministry's Web site as one of the top five hits listed. To show you what I mean by this, try a Google search on the words "Episcopal" and "Princeton." If the first listing you get is not "The Episcopal Church at Princeton University" let me know right away!

Search engines are only one gateway into your Web site. Perhaps the most important gateway is your university's own Web site. Most university Web sites have a section concerning campus life, and many have a section within the campus life pages related to religious life. Encourage your university to add a place under campus life for various chaplaincies in the religious life section on its Web site. Make sure it links to your Web site.

## Posters, Ads, and Banners

When I first became chaplain at Princeton I had to overcome a great deal of resistance among Episcopal students to do any kind of advertising in the university's daily newspaper. Similarly, there was a great reluctance to place posters around campus. My colleagues in the Methodist, Presbyterian, and Lutheran chaplaincies reported similar resistance in their groups.

This was all very confusing for me since Princeton, like all campuses, is awash in posters promoting everything from lectures by visiting heads of state and Nobel Prize winners to concerts to sandwiches at a local greasy takeout joint. When I asked what the resistance was all about I was told, "We don't want to be like *them*." "Them" turned out to be a very aggressive evangelical Christian group that had a recent history of newspaper ads and posters that threatened eternal damnation for anyone who refused their entreaties to accept Jesus Christ as personal lord and savior. These ads were seen as intolerant and as so offensive and off-putting that, in the minds of our students, *any* ad promoting a religious organization or service, no matter how welcoming and benign, would cause embarrassment and run the risk of the Episcopal Church at Princeton University being seen as all of a piece with the particular group on campus that engaged in offensive advertising.[37]

I respected the wishes of my student leaders up to a point. But I nonetheless gently pushed for using ads in the newspaper using "soft" and welcoming messages. The first ad we used became our most popular one and one that became well known around campus. It showed a modern-looking graphic of the Last Supper with a headline that read, "Absolute faith is not a requirement in our church...an open heart and mind are." At the bottom of the ad appeared the time and place of our weekly worship service along with our Web site address. Because of its high recognition value, we include the Episcopal shield on all ads.

We now vary our ads with different messages keyed to the time of the year. For example, each February the university's limited-membership eating clubs begin the "bicker" process (Princeton's version of rushing) for sophomores, the result of which is either that a person is accepted into a club or is rejected, which is called being "hosed." Being hosed is a traumatic experience, and the fear of being hosed is the source of tremendous stress for sophomores. So in late January and early February, we run ads with the familiar Last Supper graphic but with a headline that reads, "*No* bicker...*No* rush...*Nobody* gets hosed...*Everyone* is welcome!" These ads are always noticed and elicit a few laughs, favorable comments, and a jump in attendance at our weekly Eucharist.

The key thing is to vary the message and experiment with different approaches, but it is important to stick with an ad for a while until it gets noticed. Advertising can be expensive not so much because of the cost of a single ad, but because of the necessity of running ads

Blank poster        With superimposed copy

for a long period of time. To run just one ad without follow-up ads is usually a waste of money because it will not have any effect. Using attractive graphics and type fonts that have a consistent look and feel will assure that new messages are associated in people's minds with your ministry. Think of the familiar graphics of companies like Federal Express, Johnson & Johnson, and General Electric. While ads may vary, the basic identifying logo, typeface, and style remain the same and are thus immediately recognizable.

As newspaper ads became acceptable we began to use posters. Once again, we chose to stick with something easily recognizable as "Episcopal" by using the red, white, and blue eight-and-a-half-by-eleven-inch "The Episcopal Church Welcomes You" posters.[38] These posters have a blank blue bar at the bottom where worship times and places can be printed very inexpensively. We simply make up a message for the blue part of the poster in a word processing program, take it to a photocopy shop, and have them printed up in bulk on the preprinted red, white, and blue stock posters. The posters cost about ten cents apiece and five cents each for the copying. We then place them all over campus and periodically refresh them when they get torn down or weathered. We make a special effort to place these posters in every dormitory entrance on campus in September and January.

We have a distinct preference for "The Episcopal Church Welcomes You" poster as opposed to the more lukewarm "The Episcopal Church Is Here for You" poster. The latter seems to have the hidden message that we're here, but you have to find us, and we're not going to do much to help you find us! Many denominations have similar resources available through their national church headquarters, but the wise chaplain will make sure something developed by the national church will work locally on his or her own campus. Many denominational church groups have similar stock posters you can use with your own message, and you can easily devise your own. The Presbyterian campus ministry at Princeton recently began a poster campaign using the very familiar logo of the Presbyterian Church USA — a stylized cross with flames leaping up from its base. But instead of using the church's customary red, white, and blue color scheme, they cleverly substituted Princeton's orange and black color scheme. Remember, also, the discussion in chapter 1 about using familiar church logos and emblems rather than designing your own.

Another variation on the poster idea is a large plastic sandwich board that we place in front of the University Chapel on Sundays that says "Service Tonight at 10:00 in the Chapel — Communion with Music." We chose the words carefully — "service" and "communion" instead of "Eucharist." This is because not everyone knows what a Eucharist is, but nearly everyone knows what a service is, and most Christian people have an idea of what communion is about. The wording is thus intended to be as welcoming and as easily understood as possible. Again, the idea is that we are not so much targeting Episcopal "insiders" — or insiders of any Christian group — as we are those who are completely "unchurched" and may be looking for something in the way of worship and spirituality.

> **Service tonight
> at 10:00
> in the Chapel**
> ──────────
> **Communion
> with Music**
>
> *Everyone Welcome!*
>
> The **E**piscopal
> **C**hurch at
> **P**rinceton
> University

There are, besides "Eucharist," many words that only insiders recognize. An effective advertising or poster campaign will eschew jargon and use words that nearly anyone will know. Here are a few examples:

| Church Jargon | A Better Choice |
| --- | --- |
| Eucharist | Service |
| Koinonia | Community |
| Oratory | Prayer Room |
| Compline | Night Prayer |
| Vespers | Evening Prayer |
| Fellowship | Social gathering, social time |
| Lectionary | Bible readings |

Finally, we come to banners. Banners for special events and worship services can be very effective ways of bringing people in. We use a banner for our annual alumni brunch the last weekend of May. On the weekend before the brunch, we put it on the porch of the house where our ministry is located. Our most successful banner is the one for our early-morning Easter Vigil service. We place a two-sided banner over a heavily trafficked walkway on campus on Palm Sunday afternoon and another one on the porch at our building on the other side of campus. It reads "Easter Sunrise Service — 5:00 a.m. in the Chapel — Everyone welcome! — The Episcopal Church at Princeton University." Once again, the wording is deliberate: not everyone knows what an Easter Vigil is (and they don't know what they're missing!), but everyone knows, or can easily imagine, the meaning of "sunrise service." This banner resulted in a 25 percent increase in attendance at our Easter Vigil service the first year we used it.

An attractive banner on the side of a church that is very close to a college campus that reads something like: "Students! Prayers and Sandwiches every Thursday at Noon. Everyone welcome!" could bring in students who walk by the church every day without knowing that there is anything there for them. Vinyl banners created on a home computer and then printed inexpensively by an on-demand printer are both durable and a great investment.

## E-Mail and Instant Messaging

I know a chaplain who has not checked his e-mail since 1997 and has never sent an e-mail message. This same chaplain wonders why so few students come to his services and why hardly anyone ever contacts him about a pastoral concern. He says he is of a generation that communicates by telephone or face to face or not at all. Though I am older than he is, I understand that for the generation of students in university now, e-mail and instant messaging are as natural ways of communicating as speaking with someone in the same room. It is difficult to imagine a chaplain being an effective herald who does not use e-mail and instant messaging in the way that students do.

This method of communication requires checking incoming e-mail several times a day. It means learning how to compose brief, compact messages and being comfortable with a style of communication long on essential information and short on the courtesies of notes and letters written on paper, accurate spelling, good grammar, and even punctuation. One of our students began studying the New Testament in Greek and was amused and delighted to learn that it was originally written the same way she writes all her e-mails — with no punctuation and no capital letters. It also means being comfortable having an extended conversation on sensitive and difficult issues via e-mail and instant messaging, since this is how students naturally communicate.

E-mail can also be an effective way to announce weekly worship and other events. But care must be taken not to contribute to the massive amounts of unwanted and annoying e-mail that almost everyone with an e-mail account receives hourly. Our practice is to send a weekly e-mail with information about upcoming services, Bible study, special-interest groups, and anything else that needs to be communicated to our e-mail lists. We also have an iron-clad rule that we will never send more than one e-mail per week, and we assure our constituencies of this regularly.

Announcement e-mails are sent to the subscribers of our several lists. There is a separate list for each of the following:

- Each class (i.e., freshmen, sophomores, juniors, seniors)
- Postgraduate students
- Faculty
- University staff
- Friends (i.e., everyone else)
- Student leaders of the ministry

These lists can be managed by a list serve capability maintained by the university's computer services department. If your university does not have such a capability or if campus ministries do not have access to it, then you can go to a commercial provider of list servers such as LISTSERV.[39] Our policy allows any subscriber to be removed from the list at any time simply by requesting or by allowing them to do it themselves electronically, with instructions provided for doing so. As with any mailing list, it will take some work to assure that the list is current by making changes in e-mail addresses, removing addresses that result in "undelivered mail" messages, and adding new names.

People who receive a great many e-mail announcements (this includes virtually *every* student) can become inured to the content of even the most critical and interesting messages. Thus, it makes sense to vary the format and even the color of the text from time to time. It is also important to be clear what your message is about in the subject line, especially for your subscribers who may not attend your services very often or not at all. For example, if your subject line says "MCM this week," instead of "Methodist Campus Ministry this week" many people may have no idea who or what you are and may delete the message before reading it. In a similar vein, whenever you use an acronym like MCM, it is always a good practice to spell out the name of your organization the first time you use it and then go to the acronym. Don't assume everyone will know, because only the "in group" will and you will not reach the others. Student leaders who are used to referring to your ministry by its acronym will need to be reminded of this good practice quite often. Insiders refer to the Episcopal Church at Princeton University as "ECP." This acronym is problematic since it can also refer to Princeton's "Eating Concerns Program" (a program that deals with eating disorders), an Internet mathematics journal called "Electronic Communications in Probability," or to the Emergency Contraceptive Pill (the so-called morning-after-pill).

In the chapter on chaplain as steward we discussed the computerized list of alumni and friends who are reached periodically for fund-raising purposes. Many software programs for storing and retrieving names and addresses also have a mass e-mail capability, which can be used to good effect. We typically use the alumni e-mail list twice a year. Just before Ash Wednesday we send an e-mail urging people to remember our ministry in their wills (dust to dust!), and in May we invite alumni to our annual alumni brunch. Here again, it is best not to use this capability too often so as not to be annoying and likewise to remove names promptly whenever asked.

## Brochures and Newsletters

The chaplain can also communicate with various constituencies by printed media. A well-designed and informative brochure can be distributed to incoming students and left on tables and in racks at strategic locations where it can be picked up by passers-by. A brochure can tell what the chaplaincy is about and when and where its main weekly worship and fellowship events are held. It can also contain current contact information with the chaplain's telephone number and e-mail address as well as the organization's Web site address. Indeed, *every* publication — brochures, newsletters, Web sites, business cards, letterheads, and posters — should contain this important information so that each publication can reinforce every other one. An effective brochure will contain a welcoming message with an inviting tone, and it will also be intriguing in a way that prompts further investigation. For example, the brochure might say, "The Presbyterian community at the University of Anywhere is one of the university's best-kept secrets — and one you'll be glad to know about!"

Whereas brochures distributed on campus are addressed primarily to students, faculty, and staff, newsletters are primarily addressed to those who are not part of the current campus community, such as alumni and the friends and families of students. Brochures and newsletters both are intended to create awareness on the part of their various audiences. If the brochure is designed to make people aware of the chaplaincy so that they will participate in worship and fellowship, the newsletter seeks to create awareness of the chaplaincy's programs so that readers will support the ministry with their donations and with their prayers.

Newsletters should be sent out at least annually, perhaps at the start of the academic year, and should be as professionally designed and printed as resources allow. The argument is often heard that a beautifully designed and nicely printed full-color brochure will convey an unintended message that the ministry is not in need of financial support, whereas a simple black-and-white affair suggests an air of dignified poverty that induces increased giving. This has not been my experience. On the contrary, improvements in the quality of our annual newsletter have been associated year after year with increases in the number and size of donations. Perhaps the best approach is a color glossy four-page newsletter at the beginning of the year that contains an appeal for donations and includes an addressed remittance envelope followed by two or three more black-and-white two-page updates that provide news only and no requests for funds.

The newsletter is an opportunity to announce and celebrate all of the previous year's or quarter's accomplishments and events. Have you had an impressive array of inspiring guest preachers? Has attendance at your Easter service increased dramatically over last year's? Has there been a bumper crop of baptisms and confirmations? Have students from your ministry given generously of their time to an after-school tutoring program for disadvantaged children? Are you sponsoring a recent graduate for ordination? Are your students mobilized to speak out against a particular injustice on campus or in the world? Did your group go on a service trip to Central America during spring break? Alumni and parents enjoy reading such inspiring stories!

In the course of a busy year it is easy to forget all the good things that happen in a vibrant campus ministry. Thus, I find it helpful to keep a file with ideas for stories, lists of guest speakers and preachers, reminders of important milestones and accomplishments, and other items that could fill space and entertain and enlighten your readership. I was recently amazed at the impressive list of guest speakers we had had during the academic year when I undertook the task of gathering all the information in one place for our newsletter. I had been so busy during the year that I had failed to notice what wonderful speakers we had enjoyed all year long. Our readers were similarly impressed.

Brochures and newsletters should always contain plenty of photographs that reinforce the message. Particular emphasis is best given to photographs that show students doing something related to the campus ministry — working at a soup kitchen, preparing a meal, worshiping together, enjoying a football game as a group. Photographs of people doing things are always more appealing than photographs of buildings or other inanimate objects, or posed pictures of large groups, or of the chaplain. In addition to photographs, brief testimonials about the campus ministry written by students and recent graduates are extremely compelling and help to tell a story that other narratives cannot match. Finally, including relevant Bible quotation is a very useful way to remind our readers and ourselves that all we do is centered on God and the proclamation of the gospel.

## Leadership Meetings

To avoid a chaplain hearing only his or her own voice, it's useful and invigorating to be quite deliberate about sharing ideas about the campus ministry with groups, whether of student leaders or the ministry's governing body. These meetings are another way for the chaplain to function as herald. Moreover, these meetings provide an opportunity for everyone involved to share the function of herald by communicating information to the group and by sharing ideas for improving the ministry and for reexamining its mission and focus.

Regular meetings of the governing body and of the student leadership group that are chaired by someone other than the chaplain can guard against a dangerous tendency, namely, over a long tenure a chaplain can come to believe — albeit unconsciously — that he or she owns the chaplaincy. The governing board and the students are often complicit in this sense that the chaplain owns the ministry and that they have little or no say in how things ought to be.

At Princeton we have found that weekly meetings of the principal student leaders of the ministry work best, with the cabinet meeting monthly and the governing board meeting monthly, but no more infrequently than quarterly. We keep careful public records with agendas and minutes of each meeting. The minutes of the previous meeting are reviewed and approved at the beginning of each meeting, and items for follow-up are noted and acted upon.

## Guest Speakers and Preachers

A chaplain's effectiveness as a herald is enhanced by inviting others to share the burden. Having occasional guest preachers at regular worship and guest speakers at weekly fellowship gatherings can have a number of benefits: it exposes students to experts in their subjects or to ideas that may be different from, or even in opposition to, those held by the chaplain; it exposes them to various points of view regarding issues in the larger church; and it helps students see how they and their local campus ministry are an integral part of the worldwide church of God. Also, the chaplain will want to expose students to voices of people who differ from the chaplain in terms of race, color, and gender. These opportunities welcome intellectual and spiritual challenge and growth for the chaplain as well as the students.

The Episcopal Church at Princeton University has long practiced open communion at its worship services. Any and all are invited to share in holy communion, whether baptized or not. This stance is controversial within the Episcopal Church, and it contravenes the canons — official positions and rules — of our church, yet it has been seen as a very positive feature of our common life. However, in the spring of 2004 an article appeared in the leading Anglican theological journal calling open communion into question by examining the relationship between baptism and the Eucharist in a very thoughtful and thought-provoking way. In the next issue of the same journal an opposing view was expressed — one consistent with our long-standing practice. In the fall of 2004 we invited one of the authors of these papers to come to Princeton to present his views and help us think through this issue as thoroughly as possible, and we intend to invite others. As I write this our students are still engaged in the process of working through this issue. But I am confident that in the end, whether we retain the practice of open communion or not, our ministry will be on more solid theological ground than we were before these authors visited Princeton.

Finally, guest preachers and speakers assist the chaplain in providing biblically and theologically illiterate students — and faculty and staff — with a sound foundation of biblical preaching and theological basics. The more sophisticated conversations about important matters that ensue affirm that such efforts pay rich dividends in the church's future.

Every chaplain will exercise the office of herald in ways that best suit his or her own gifts and the particular circumstances of the university the ministry serves. The foregoing are intended to point the way toward some of the key elements of this office and offer a few ideas that have worked well in Princeton and elsewhere. The main point, though, is to ensure that the gospel is proclaimed and that our ministry to the campus is not hidden under a bushel basket but is visible, welcoming, and engaging to the entire community. However, within the campus and in the world at large there are those who have never truly heard the good news of Jesus Christ. In the next chapter we expand our vision to the world beyond the ministry itself.

# Chapter 7

# The Chaplain as Missionary

*One who is sent out or sent forth; one who conducts a mission.*

———— ✠ ————

**I** HAVE A NEIGHBOR who enjoys doing projects around his house. Don's drive and passion for his projects is such that it excites and engages others in working on projects with him. I think God is like that about God's own project — the main thing God wants to accomplish with us, through us, and, especially, for us.

God's project is about a lot of things, but most important and especially it is about announcing the inbreaking of God into the world through Jesus Christ. Matthew's Gospel (chapter 28) famously addresses this project right at the end where Jesus gives his great commission to go out and spread the good news to all people in his name. Christianity is an evangelical religion: it demands to be shared and spread. The news is too good, too amazing, too wonderful to keep to ourselves. In the same way that we don't need to be told to alert a friend to a great new piece of music or a new restaurant, we all have an inner desire to share what has given us joy and meaning in our lives. In a world starved for meaning, for peace and justice, and especially for love that never fails or falters, the good news of Jesus Christ is the best news there is. Wilbert Shenk asserts that announcing this good news to the world is so basic to what the church is by quoting Emil Brunner's famous adage, "The church exists by mission, just as fire exists by burning."[40]

There is something about a university community, influenced as it is by the Enlightenment, modernism, secularism, and postmodernism, that resists not only the good news itself but even the necessity of hearing it. Thus, the challenge for the Christian on campus is to be a part of the university while offering it a message it may not want to hear. The university campus is a rich mission field, and campus ministry is an expression of the church's eagerness to be a part of the lives of all those involved with the university.

The Christian chaplain must be a missionary to the university and, in keeping with a theme that has run throughout this book, must educate, equip, and engage others to do the same. The chaplain must, in short, take seriously Jesus' great commission and encourage others to take it to heart as well. That commission, of course, also extends to places beyond the campus where Christ is unknown or where Christianity in under siege, even places far, far away. But let us not neglect our mission right here at home, right on the university campus. Even so close to home, Christ is unknown to many.

In some ways the challenge to be a missionary in a place where we live and work is even more difficult than the challenge of taking the good news of Christ to a far-off place. After all, if we are rejected by people we don't know and with whom we will never again have to interact or upon whom we will never have to depend for career advancement, such rejection is easier to bear than rejection by those with whom we live and upon whom we depend for our futures.

The great commission in Matthew tells us *what* to do as missionaries to the world, but not *how* to do it. We are left with the feeling that we are on the hook for something big and important, but a little unsure about how to proceed. For that we can turn to Luke's Gospel. Whereas Jesus in Matthew 28 gives the great commission only to the remaining eleven disciples, seventy disciples are commissioned in Luke 10. This seems to indicate that mission is the work not of a few, but of everyone. We are all expected to go out, "two by two," spreading the good news. Then Luke's Jesus gives detailed and explicit instructions to the seventy, instructions that are clear and readily adaptable to every time and place. So, let's play back the tape

and hear Jesus' own words (Luke 10:2–12) for how to be a missionary and think of their application to mission and evangelism on a
university campus.[41]

First Jesus says, "The harvest is plentiful. . . . " He affirms that there
is a need for mission, that there is plenty of work to do. And he
suggests that there are not enough workers to bring in the harvest.
Indeed, the chaplain as missionary can at times feel overwhelmed by
the magnitude of the task. For every person who attends worship
services or who begins to show some interest in learning about God's
project, there are a hundred or more for whom such matters are the
furthest thing from their minds, and there are even a few who are
outright hostile to the good news of Jesus Christ. The roots of this
hostility may give us a clue about how to be a missionary church.
David J. Bosch points out that churches are empty not necessarily
because the tenets of Christianity are unacceptable to the modern
world.[42] They are empty because of the apparent disconnect between
what Jesus said and what we actually do. Collectively, we do not have
a very good track record, Bosch says. If we preach love and practice
hate, we will not win anyone to Christ.

We have tried to help one another notice whenever the church
on campus is not being consistent with the gospel message. In our
leadership group meetings we ask ourselves whether we could do a
better job of being Christian witnesses. Are we silent about evidence
of bigotry when we should be speaking out? Does our budget reflect
a true Christian message when expenses for our fellowship dinners
exceed expenses for mission activities and donations to help others?
Do we say we are a welcoming church and then ignore newcomers
to our services? By asking ourselves these questions and by facing the
issues squarely, we begin to bridge whatever gap exists between what
we preach and what we really do.

Then Jesus says, "Ask the lord of the harvest. . . . " Here he reminds us of the importance of prayer to the church's mission. We
have touched in other chapters on this fundamental necessity of beginning and ending everything in prayer. To be sure, some students

are wary of praying for mission on campus because they do not wish to espouse a view that anyone who has not "accepted Jesus Christ as their personal savior" is in deep eschatological trouble. Here the chaplain's job is to show that praying for God to help us be missionaries is not an implied condemnation of those who cannot or will not hear God's good news. I have had success in this area by asking students who have a gift for leading prayer to do so and to focus on prayers for mission. Such prayers by peers have a power that my prayer as chaplain might not have.

"Go your own way, ... " Jesus says next. Here he is telling the disciples that each one of them has a role to play and that, moreover, each one of them is expected to participate in this great project, contributing to the enterprise whatever and however one is capable of contributing. Paul's riff in 1 Corinthians (12:4–11) about varieties of spiritual gifts comes to mind here. Some may spread the good news by being a caring friend to a lonely or troubled classmate. Others may be able to witness to Christ through athletic endeavors. Still others may join in on campuswide service projects or in protests against injustice, and in subtle but unabashed ways make it clear that their motivation is following the loving example of Jesus. Others may find ways in the classroom to be clear and open about their faith. At Princeton we have examples in our current and previous student groups of each of these ways to minister and many others as well. We work hard to recognize and affirm these differences by offering public prayers of thanksgiving for various student ministries, and student leaders are always alert to possible ways of holding up various types of ministry as examples to others.

Next Jesus gives the warning, "I am sending you out like lambs into the midst of wolves. ... " It is as if Jesus is telling the committed Christian members of the university community that he understands that they will feel some reluctance to be *too* open about being one of his followers in an environment that may be not only unwelcoming, but even punishing. Graduate students and junior faculty members are particularly vulnerable to fears that being openly Christian may limit their academic careers, but even undergraduates may feel the chill of secular disdain for Christ. But by acknowledging the reality of the likely reception his followers will receive, Jesus is simultaneously restating the challenge. The difficulty of the task — even its impossibility — is not a reason to shrink from it! Here, too, we have had good experiences with group discussions that allow students to share with their peers the joys and frustrations of trying to be a Christian witness on campus. These peer group conversations can strengthen everyone's resolve through mutual encouragement.

Jesus then admonishes the seventy to "greet no one on the road." Here, I think, he is saying, "Stay focused! Keep your eye on the mission. Don't get distracted!" In the American South, there is a saying that goes, "The main thing is always to keep the main thing the main thing." There is much that passes for Christianity and yet is unrelated to the main message of Jesus Christ. Complicated, confused, and contradictory messages are difficult for anyone to hear — even clever university students — and they have no place in missionary discourse! The Jesus Christ of the Gospels is an incredibly attractive and compelling figure. Here Jesus seems to be telling us, "When you speak of me to others on the university campus, keep it clear and simple. Talk about love of God and love of neighbor and encourage prayer. That's enough for beginners. The rest will take care of itself." At Princeton we attempt to address this issue by resisting the temptation to use our Wednesday evening programs to go too far afield with topics. So, for example, instead of a random collection of discussions on relatively unimportant forms of church ritual, political squabbles within the church on minor issues, and whether or not incense should be used throughout the church year, we try to focus our limited time together on "the basics" — the meaning of the creeds, what we mean by the Trinity, how to pray, how to make moral choices, and other fundamental issues that equip our students to build up the church.

Jesus now comes to the punch line. He says, "Say 'Peace to this house' and . . . 'The Kingdom of God is near to you.' " The idea that God is very close to us and that God is easily accessible to each one of us was a radical idea in Jesus' time, and the sad truth is that it still is. How many opportunities there are in an ordinary day at a typical university for one who knows that God is near to share this wonderful news! There are many places where God can seem very far away. University communities, because of the way that they prize intellectual accomplishments, can be an environment even more oblivious to the nearness of God than a prison or a hospital ward. It has dawned on many prisoners and patients not only that they need God, but also that God is quite near to them in a way that many academics — dare I say, in their arrogance — would find surprising. The trouble is that many academics would also find this realization quaint. But the notion of the nearness and availability of God to your typical academic might be less quaint and odd if it were obviously and explicitly the belief of a respected and admired classmate, teammate, professor, or administrator. I can think of several such people at Princeton who are powerful witnesses to Christ as a result of their secular accomplishments combined with the fact that they are quite open about their faith and unashamed to acknowledge their faith publicly. One manifestation that springs to mind is a student I know who always can be relied upon to ask another person how they are doing and about their family. Often this sincere and genuine display of concern — which, of course, is itself powerfully Christ-like — will elicit news of a family illness, trouble with a boyfriend, a struggle with schoolwork, or some other troubling matter. This then always results in this young woman saying, "I'll pray for you. Will you pray for me too?"

Then Jesus says, "Eat what is set before you. . . . " Here, Culpepper suggests, Jesus wants to make it clear that it is the host, not the guest who sets the context for the witness to Christ. We must encounter others wherever they are. We must engage in mission not on our terms and with our own agenda and vocabulary, but on the terms of the others to whom we seek to introduce God's good news. Whenever we discuss evangelism — good news — at Princeton, we speak of it not so much as something that is offered to another as a response to something a person has expressed.

Then Jesus takes up the problem, " ... [W]henever ... they do not welcome you, ... " as if to inoculate the disciples against disappointment. By giving them a response to being unwelcome he prepares them for those times when their best efforts will seem to be in vain. I am often called upon to soothe the hurt feelings and bruised egos of disciples who, in the fervor and enthusiasm that is one of the more salutary and lovable marks of youth, cannot imagine why their witness so often falls on deaf ears or is rejected with either hostility or condescension. In these cases I try to remember to remind the disciples of Jesus' next words about wiping the dust from their feet by way of encouraging them to persevere in spite of setbacks and rejection. Here again, a way to promote missionary activity on campus that works for us is to talk about it as often as we can — to be intentional about being missionaries and about what it takes to help others see and hear Christ's good news through us.

Finally, Jesus once more comes back to the main thing when he says, "Yet know this, the kingdom of God has come near you." After preparing the disciples for disappointment, he calls their attention to God's project and assures them of God's redemptive presence in the world.

Offering Bible study groups, providing opportunities for service in Christ's name (volunteering at a Habitat for Humanity project, a local homeless shelter, after-school tutoring for inner-city children, and the like), a quiet conversation about faith with a friend, and a simple openness about being a Christian (such as letting roommates and other friends know when you're going to church and inviting them to come along) are all ways to be a missionary on a university campus. Exactly how God's nearness can best be announced in different academic settings and how members of the university community can be helped to recognize God's nearness is something each chaplain will have to explore within the context of the local Christian community. But from age to age and place to place the basis of God's redemptive love is, thanks be to God, constant. Mission for each campus ministry will be worked out with this assurance.

Finally, we return to the concept of simply showing up. One effective way for a chaplain to be a missionary is to be visible on campus. I was recently invited to attend a good-bye party for a senior administrator at Princeton who had accepted the presidency of another university. I was not quite sure why I had been invited because I did not know the departing administrator, and I considered not going. But in the end I did go because I knew the university president would be there, and her presence would attract many other key people. I decided that this would be a place where I could be a witness to Christ at Princeton just by showing up and that my presence would be a tacit reminder to the university's decision makers that there is a spiritual dimension to the university that can coexist with the life of the mind.

St. Francis of Assisi is supposed to have said, "Preach the gospel at all times, and when necessary use words." By our actions others will know we are Christians and that we are for real. By caring for one another within the campus ministry group and by looking beyond the group for ways we can serve others we will be true missionaries not by what we say but by what we do. In this way we will alert first ourselves, and then others, to the universal reign of God.

Let's turn now to the chaplain as pilgrim and examine how the chaplain is sustained and sustains others on the lifelong journey toward God.

Chapter 8

# The Chaplain as Pilgrim

*One who makes a spiritual journey.*

———— ✠ ————

I FELL INTO the queue at the campus store behind Jennifer as she was placing into her book bag the can of Red Bull she had just purchased. This high-octane drink is loaded with caffeine, taurine, glucuronolactone, and sugar, and its manufacturer says that it improves performance and concentration, especially during times of stress. The campus store can't seem to keep enough of it on the shelves.

This was the second time that day I had seen Jennifer. We met for morning coffee — she had the twenty-ounce French roast — during which she was dolefully reviewing her schedule. "I don't have time for anything," she lamented. She had only slept for a couple of hours each of the previous three nights. In addition to a heavy load of classes she held significant leadership roles in three campus organizations and was in the process of interviewing with several Wall Street firms for a job following graduation.

Jennifer waved away my concern saying, "Everybody does this. In fact, I've got it easy compared to some of my friends." When I asked her how long she thought she could keep this up, she first made the excuse that the winter holidays were coming soon and she would get a rest then. Then she looked down and said, "But this can't go on. It's really insane!" I gently reminded her that it is useful to think of life more as a long journey than a short sprint — or even a series of sprints.

Jennifer's life lacks balance. This seems to be a condition of modern society that determines how college students conduct their lives. Many of them have been conditioned from a very early age to achieve all they can academically and socially. Their achievements provide opportunities to begin new races for other achievements with the field of competitors becoming smaller and the competition more intense. The striving drives out opportunities to reflect, rest, deeply enjoy the company of another, and pray. Desmond Tutu calls this the "idolatry of busyness."

This metaphor of life as a spiritual journey explains why some students are drawn to a campus ministry. They seek to be more intentional about finding a sense of balance while they are on their journey, but are confused, bewildered, and unsure of how to proceed. Indeed, the desire for guidance in finding this balance may be the single greatest motivator in drawing students and others to whatever the campus ministry has to offer.

The life of a university chaplain can be a model of a balanced life for others. Instead of modeling super achievement, the chaplain as pilgrim can be a person on a deliberate, purposeful spiritual journey — an imperfect, flawed person striving nonetheless for perfection not in the résumé-building sense, but in the spiritual sense. Students, as well as faculty and staff, need leadership in making their own spiritual journey. By being diligent about being on his or her own journey, the chaplain will have great authority in leading others on theirs. This cannot be faked or put on. If the chaplain's attempt to live a balanced life is not genuine, not part of the true self and of daily practice, then it quickly will be detected as fraudulent.

A chaplain is a companion with students, faculty, and staff on the spiritual journey. Conveying a sense of togetherness and community in the spiritual journey is critically important, to be sure. And it is a commonplace that Christianity is very much a religion of community in which the lifelong spiritual journey toward God is undertaken in the company of other pilgrims. As prayer is so basic and essential to the spiritual life, let's begin there.

## Daily Prayer

Before I went to seminary I spent many years as a business executive. Toward the end of my business career I felt like an imposter most of the time, and although I functioned well at work, I knew deep down that I was in the wrong place, doing things that I was not really called to do. The feeling that I was faking it made simple tasks seem insurmountable.

When I left business and entered seminary, I thought the feeling of faking it was a thing of the past for me; for a while it was. In seminary I was in the company of others who were trying to observe a daily routine of prayer, and this supported my own prayer discipline. I felt connected with others and with God in a way I had never known before, and I experienced a feeling of real authenticity that I had previously only glimpsed.

After ordination things began to change. I no longer could rely on the comfortable and supportive routine of seminary life that was built around daily common prayer. Now I had to work my prayer life into the demands of life as a husband, father, and minister. My prayer life was something I had to struggle to maintain on my own. The big surprise was that when it slipped and I found myself going several days or even a week without saying my prayers, the feeling of being an imposter came back with a vengeance!

I've never asked anyone if they could discern a difference in me between those times when I was keeping up with daily prayer and those when I was not. But I'm sure they could.

Being on a spiritual journey — being a pilgrim — is really a striving for personal holiness. This striving for holiness, when it is in full blossom, manifests itself in how one relates, in love, to others. But it does not begin there. Love of neighbor in the deepest Christian sense begins with love of God, not the other way around. During those times when I am faithful to my prayer I am, as a result, more aware of my love for God and God's love for me. This awareness in turn results in my experience of love for others. Prayer, in other words, makes me a better priest.

My struggles to get back this feeling of connectedness to God and to others is most successful when I can re-create some of the structure that life in seminary provides. I find that a habit of prayer in which I pray in the same location using the same format on a daily basis can make me, when it is going well, full of grace and peace. I sit in the same chair in a quiet room and use the daily office of the *Book of Common Prayer.* Similar forms of daily prayer are found in other traditions and nearly always rely on the book of Psalms as their core. Regular prayer based on the Psalms can make hardships and afflictions of all kinds bearable for me. The opposite is true when I fall out of these habits. Then I become irritable more easily, I lose patience with those who seek my help and counsel, and I feel as though I am just going through the motions of ministry with no feeling for it whatever. Alas, before long others begin to notice too.

Only when we reach this stage of grasping the depth of God's love through prayer do we naturally become aware — almost simultaneously — of our deep love for others, for neighbor. Then we are able to be leaders for others on their pilgrimages. Being a person of prayer is about much more than merely being a role model for others. It is about having our own spiritual fuel and energy that makes all other aspects of ministry possible.

In my second year of ministry I found that every time a certain student asked to speak with me I would become uneasy and even a bit resentful. Richard held theological and political views that were very different from mine, and I found his interpersonal style to be grating and at times even offensive. I had not wanted to admit it to myself, but I finally did admit that the truth was that I just didn't like him very much. About the same time I realized that my prayer life had dried up. So I began to pray for Richard. And as soon as I did it did not take long for me to realize that in spite of all our differences, and in spite of qualities in him that I did not like, he really was just like me in all the important ways — human and beloved of God. I could not have come to this realization if I had not begun to pray for him, and if I had not realized this I could not have been — and continue to be — Richard's companion on his spiritual journey.

## Regular Retreats

In medieval times there was a good deal of discussion about what helped or hindered the spiritual life. One of the things that hindered the spiritual journey was *curae*, or the cares and concerns of life in the "the world." *Curae* might be thought of as another way of referring to a life that is out of balance, off kilter. A way of avoiding *curae* was to withdraw from the world and to take up the monastic life, a life protected from *curae* that could be given over completely to prayer and the quest for spiritual perfection and the peace it brings. It was, in the literal sense, a retreat from the world in which a person could engage in a daily rhythm of prayer, study, work, and rest whose sole focus was a deeper knowledge of and relationship with God.

Some people are still called to a life apart from *curae* though most of us are not.[43] Nonetheless, anyone who is serious about the spiritual journey that *is* the Christian life can benefit from periodic respite from the cares and concerns of a hectic modern life. Indeed, Jesus himself is our model for this when after a particularly busy time he went off himself to a lonely place for prayer and rest. A change of daily routine in a different venue that is conducive to prayer and contemplation, preferably in a beautiful place, can help recharge and reenergize our spiritual lives by helping us refocus and by helping us return to a prayer life that may have begun to be fallow.

My first experience of such a retreat was as a high school student when a priest in my church took me to visit a Roman Catholic Benedictine priory in the hills of Vermont. I was awestruck by the beauty of the place combined with the directness and simplicity of the worship. It seemed that every aspect of the place played a part in drawing my mind and heart toward God. I continued to visit this place for many years and later formed a relationship with an Anglican Benedictine monastery on the banks of the Hudson River in New York where I have taken Princeton students on retreat.

Monasteries and convents make it their business to provide hospitality to weary souls. College students almost universally experience a monastic retreat to be a life-changing experience. Each year when we begin recruiting students to attend our spring retreat at the monastery in New York we ask students who have been before to tell others what it is like. One of the biggest selling points for driven, ambitious, Red Bull–drinking Princeton students is that they can bring their academic work along with them to the monastery.

I first asked Cynthia to come along on a retreat when she was a freshman. She felt she was just too busy to spend a weekend away from Princeton, as appealing as the idea was. She gave the same reply when I invited her in her second and third years. Midway through her senior year she came to me one day in tears saying she could not see how she could possibly finish her senior thesis in time because she was so overwhelmed by all her commitments, especially the thesis. So once again I suggested she come away with us to the monastery and this time she agreed to come, probably because she felt she was at the end of her rope anyway. During the weekend retreat Cynthia came to each of the five daily worship times, attended all the conferences, went for walks by the river with friends, and never missed a meal. And in the van on the trip home she announced to one and all, "I finished my thesis this morning! I can't believe how much work I got done here." She later told me how spiritually "connected" she felt with God, with everyone else, and with what she described as "my true self."

Those who have never been on a retreat find it unbelievable, as Cynthia once did, that they will get more studying and writing done at the monastery than they ever can accomplish during a weekend at Princeton. They also think it is odd that it would be a good thing to take work with them on retreat. Cynthia was astonished to discover the paradox that the balance of prayer, silence, study, rest, and relaxation that she experienced on the retreat always allowed for getting more done at the monastery than at the university dormitory. In addition to all the other benefits the retreat has for the spiritual life, this model of a balanced life is something that retreat-goers try to bring back with them to "the world" as an antidote to *curae*. That's why it is a good thing to take work along. This appreciation of how life can be balanced is something that is rarely gained in a university education.

An annual retreat is a wonderful addition to a campus ministry's program. If a monastic retreat is not possible, either because there are no monasteries or convents within a reasonable distance of the university or because the idea of going to a monastery is so alien to the religious tradition of the ministry, then some other kind of retreat to a peaceful location — at the sea, on a lake, or in the mountains — can be made. In these cases, the chaplain may wish to engage the services of an experienced retreat leader, and the daily program should include periods of prayer at morning, noon, evening, and before retiring as well as periods of silence (for example, from the end of night prayer to the end of breakfast the following morning). It is the combination within a single weekend of a deliberate focus on prayer, silence while eating or just being with others, and a beautiful and peaceful environment that makes a retreat a life-changing experience; so few modern people have known these elements in their lives. Indeed, most of us have known the opposite to such an extent that we are quite numb!

The annual retreat with students can complement, not be a substitute for, the chaplain's own retreat at some other time during the year. The group time with students is a wonderful experience, but even when others are along as facilitators or retreat leaders, I always feel as though I am "on duty" during the student retreats and find that I need my own time later on. My favorite time to make a retreat is the weekend just before Christmas. This is a time when most students have left campus for the Christmas recess and my duties lighten. And it is a time when the commercial buzz of the world is at a fever pitch —

the perfect time for making a retreat to renew one's own soul. Since I began making an annual pre-Christmas retreat I have been inured to the stress that used to mark my Christmas season and have found new joy and peace in the celebration of God's incarnation.

By now you've detected my preference for monasteries. They work best for me because of their built-in daily routines and structure, and they are invariably in beautiful settings. But those with other temperaments may find unstructured time at a cabin in the woods or by the sea more congenial. A friend of mine likes to make his retreat alone by hiking portions of the Appalachian Trail, stopping seven times a day to pray the daily office from the *Roman Breviary* — "Seven times a day I praise you ... " (Ps. 119:164).

Whenever I go on retreat I take lots of books with me. Some of them are spiritual, theological, or Bible commentary books that I dip into throughout the weekend. I also take along pleasure reading — a novel or two and a stack of unread magazines that I enjoy. This way I balance — there's that word again! — my study, prayer, and relaxation. While I'm there I try to take a nap whenever I'm feeling a little sleepy, and I try to eat moderately so that I'm satisfied but not stuffed. This allows me to be mindful of the rhythms of my body and helps me slow down and get centered. I also try to exercise a couple of times a day by taking long walks. My daily routine on retreat is one of unstructured structure. What I mean is, there are regular times for prayer in the chapel, and if I want to eat I have to be at the dining room when meals are served. But otherwise I give myself permission to do whatever I feel like doing. I may not open even one of the books I brought along, but I always manage to do a lot of reading of other interesting and enriching things I find at the monastery. I always come away refreshed in body and soul.

## Spiritual Direction

Another way that a chaplain can be a fellow pilgrim with students, faculty, and staff is to serve as a spiritual director. This function has a long history in Christian spirituality. Jesus himself taught his friends how to pray and offered advice and guidance about how they should think about their relationship with God and what they should do to deepen that relationship. The desert fathers and mothers of the early church and other wise holy persons throughout the ages have served as spiritual directors to seekers as well as the spiritually sophisticated who wish to go further on their journeys.

Because of many abuses that had arisen over the centuries, the Reformation rightly rejected the notion that anyone other than Jesus Christ can be an advocate and mediator between us and God. As with any correction, some salutary ideas and practices were swept away with those that were badly in need of reform. The corrective to late medieval abuses was a reliance solely on one's own spiritual life based on private study of the Bible. Thus, even in our own day, the idea of seeking spiritual direction from someone else has been regarded with a good deal of suspicion in some Christian circles. Happily, however, we seem to be in a period of recovering this practice, as more and more people of all denominations are enlisting the help of others — ordained and unordained alike — in working on their prayer lives and their personal relationship with God. After all, if we think of the Christian life as a journey — a pilgrimage — then it stands to reason that some travelers have been on the road longer than others and have experiences and knowledge worth sharing with others.

With students I find this work often has to do with discussions of "first principles." Who is Jesus Christ for them? What is prayer? Is there a right way and a wrong way to pray? Why isn't it enough just to read the Bible? Are there prayer practices that are particularly helpful for a beginner? Are there books to read that are helpful?[44]

Sometimes spiritual direction takes the form of helping a person work through ways in which earlier experiences in the church have been damaging or hurtful. This is the quintessential good news, bad news situation. The good news is that in spite of unhappy past experiences, a person is "hanging in there" and continuing to seek a relationship with God through the church. The bad news is that they have so much to overcome, so much extra baggage to put down. In these cases, spiritual direction often takes the form of the chaplain simply saying things like, "No, that does not mean you are going to hell" or "Yes, you're right — that's a wonderful way to pray!" or "You've had such hateful things said to you in the name of the church, yet you continue to trust that God loves you and cares for you. What great progress you're making!"

Margaret Guenther has written beautifully on the subject of offering spiritual direction to others.[45] She calls the process "holy listening," and indeed that is what it is. Spiritual direction is not psychotherapy or a substitute for therapy. It has as its purpose progress in the spiritual life. To be sure, there are sometimes psychological obstacles to spiritual progress and sometimes persons ought to be referred to professional therapists and counselors. Indeed, for some people who have serious psychological problems, spiritual direction probably ought to be put off until those problems can be addressed professionally. The chaplain offering spiritual direction must be clear about the differences and be sensitive to those cases that require something other than "holy listening."

Holy listening — listening with the heart as well as the mind — and reflecting back what is heard can help a person notice progress as well as hindrances to the spiritual life. This can lead to the chaplain offering gentle suggestions that may seem appropriate such as "Perhaps if you were to pray a few psalms each morning before going to lectures, you might gain some clarity on what we've been talking about."

I met Mary Ann at the end of her second week at Princeton. She was feeling behind in biochemistry and microeconomics — two of the toughest introductory courses at Princeton. Neither was necessary for her to take, since she was sure she would major in comparative literature. When I suggested that there might be other ways for her to satisfy core course requirements other than taking these two, she responded by saying, "An educated person *should* know something about biochemistry and microeconomics." As I got to know her better I heard the word "should" many times during each of our conversations, often connected with rather harsh self-appraisals of her morality and spirituality. The more progress Mary Ann made in her spiritual life, the more she said "I should.... "

Sometimes a person on a serious, deliberate spiritual journey is troubled by what Roman Catholic moral theologians call "scruples." They seem to be noticing with a heightened and acute sensitivity all the ways that they are imperfect before God, all the ways in which they are "sinful." This seems to them to be evidence that they are making no progress at all and, indeed, that they may even be worse off than when they first began. Often these conversations are accompanied by tearful self-recriminations that can seem to be bogging the person down, as was the case with Mary Ann. It is often useful in these situations to point out that, if God is light, then becoming closer and closer to God — to the Light who is the source of all light — will inevitably illuminate the ways in which we are utterly human and quite unlike God. It then can be suggested that, far from being evidence of spiritual failure, noticing lots of imperfections is actually a very good sign of progress. This simple insight along with a little encouragement to "keep up the good work" can be extraordinarily helpful and a real lift — and gift! — to the troubled pilgrim. By the time Mary Ann graduated she was able to laugh at her by then more infrequent use of statements beginning with "I should.... "

It is obvious, but still worth saying, that the chaplain as pilgrim who offers spiritual direction to others can benefit immeasurably from his or her own spiritual direction. Shepherds must be fed and cared for, too!

I also want to say a word about a suspicion that some of my brothers and sisters who are rooted in the Reformed Christian tradition have about monastic retreats, spiritual direction, and the whole issue of spirituality in general. Among some there is a deeply held belief that spirituality and intentional spiritual practices are related to an asceticism that is grounded in works righteousness. They believe that faith alone justifies them, and working hard to develop a spiritual life is dangerously close to trying to work your way into heaven.

My first response is that spirituality is about nothing more — or less — than prayer. To work on a spiritual life is to work on a prayer life and vice versa. There are, of course, numerous biblical warrants for prayer, including the words and deeds of Jesus himself. I also want to suggest that there's nothing like trying something to see what it's really like. A few years ago administrators at Princeton Theological Seminary — a moderately conservative Presbyterian institution — overcame their suspicion of such matters by taking a group of students on a retreat at an Episcopal monastery in New York. The retreat was oversubscribed from the beginning and has been a popular annual event ever since. The seminary now makes available opportunities for group spiritual direction to those who want it.

## Relationship with the Wider Church

The mainstream life of the church is not in campus ministry, but in the parishes and congregations where people of all ages, all educational and economic backgrounds, and all walks of life come together to know Christ. Indeed, campus ministry, from a clergyperson's point of view, exists in a rarified atmosphere quite unlike what one encounters almost anywhere else. The life of a synod, diocese, presbytery, or district is organized around this reality, and the main focus of convocational meetings, annual church conventions, clergy conferences, and other meetings is usually focused on issues related to parish life. This can have the effect of making campus chaplains (not to mention hospital, prison, and school chaplains and clergy in other forms of nonparochial ministry) feel a bit out of place and even isolated, even in those cases where they are part of a parish staff. Campus ministry has, over the last thirty years, received short shrift in church budgets, which is another reason why college chaplains can feel embattled and unsupported.

It is thus critical that the chaplain maintain good relationships with the church beyond the university. One important way to do this is to be in regular contact with one's supervisor. In the Catholic tradition the bishop is every priest's and deacon's chief pastor and in the case of campus ministry is often the chaplain's direct supervisor. Similar relationships obtain in other traditions. Thus, a close working relationship with the bishop or other supervisor is vital for the chaplain's effectiveness on the job and for the chaplain's spiritual well-being. This relationship can be a significant link to the wider church.

In my tenure as a chaplain I have been blessed with the support of two different bishops who have been wonderful pastors to me. With them I have been able to speak freely about the joys and frustrations of ministry and receive valuable guidance during those dry spells in my prayer life that I mentioned earlier.

Another way to maintain these relationships is to be a part of church committees and projects outside the university, which will serve not only to keep the chaplain connected to fellow church people, but will give a wider perspective to what the work of the church is about in the world. It will also help the chaplain be alert to service and spiritual growth opportunities for students beyond the campus.

Support groups of clergy can also help to keep the chaplain connected to the wider church. These clergy peer groups come in various forms, from a book group that meets monthly to a group that meets more often and goes more deeply into the spiritual lives of its members through discussion, common prayer, and mutual support. As well, local interdenominational and interfaith clergy groups can provide rich opportunities for friendships, support, and a broadened perspective.

Most chaplains are well aware of all these opportunities to be connected and related to the wider church, yet they can become so caught up with the rarified life of the academy that they give less emphasis to these relationships outside the university than to more immediate concerns. My own involvement with the antiracism commission of my diocese and my work on dialog groups with other denominations and faiths have kept me connected with the church and the world outside Princeton. These experiences give me material that finds its way back into my ministry at Princeton in the form of sermons, conversations, networking, and visitors to our weekly dinners. They have helped me see the relationship between campus ministry and the rest of the church and have helped me keep my feet on the ground.

## Boundaries

Owing to some highly publicized abuses, there has wisely been much discussion in recent years about the importance of maintaining proper boundaries between clergy and those in our care. Some violations of boundaries have graver consequences than others. For example, for a chaplain in his or her late forties or early fifties to play at being part of the same youth culture as a university student can be less harmful than other kinds of boundary violations, but certainly can be perceived as silly and may thus diminish the chaplain's ability to be a fellow pilgrim, priest, rabbi, pastor, and so on. Indeed, rather than an impediment to campus ministry, an age difference between chaplain and students may actually enhance the chaplain's ministry. I am roughly the age of the parents of most of the students now in university. As a result I can be the wise sage for a student, whereas his or her own father might well be perceived as hopelessly out of touch and as intrusive or controlling if he offered the same advice I offer. Relationships between young adults and their parents are often fraught and sometimes even "radioactive" in a way that a chaplain-student relationship is not. But one must always be mindful that there is an age boundary, and it must be maintained.

Even more important than age boundaries are sexual boundaries. It is a commonplace that university-age young people are becoming aware of aspects of their own sexuality that may previously have been unexamined, notwithstanding the trend toward earlier and earlier sexual experimentation in adolescence. This may range from a late blossoming of sexual interest and awareness to issues of confused or evolving sexual identity. It is a safe bet to assume that sex is on the mind of any young person a good deal of the time, and that this heightened sexual awareness colors many conversations, including those on any imaginable topic with a chaplain of either gender. And that's just for starters! When conversations turn to relationships with boy- or girlfriends or to the warmth of the relationship between the chaplain and the student, both the student and the chaplain can, if not careful, begin to approach boundaries that should be observed and maintained.

It is not useful or helpful to obscure the fact that powerful sexual attractions can exist between students and chaplains, irrespective of the gender or age differences between them. Pretending that these attractions do not exist does not make them go away or make them easier to deal with. Indeed, denying to oneself that what one is feeling is sexual attraction as opposed to the more ordinary affection one can have for any other person can lead to a spiraling intensity of the attraction, and that, in turn, can lead to words and actions that can be truly damaging.

In this area of ministry, no margin exists for error and nothing is negotiable. Most denominational judicatories have clear standards regarding sexual abuse, and most require periodic training to keep clergy sensitive to all the issues. The following definitions and guidelines regarding sexual misconduct and the pastoral relationship are fairly typical.

"Sexual misconduct" means any:

a. sexual abuse or sexual molestation of any person — including but not limited to any sexual involvement or sexual contact with a person who is a minor or is legally incompetent; or

b. sexual harassment — where there is an employment, mentor, or colleague relationship between the persons involved and including but not limited to sexually oriented humor or language; questions or comments about sexual behavior or preference unrelated to employment qualifications, undesired physical contact, inappropriate comments about clothing or physical appearance, or repeated requests for social engagements; or

c. sexual exploitation — including but not limited to the development or the attempt to develop a sexual relationship between a cleric, employee, or volunteer and another adult with whom he/she has a pastoral or a superior-subordinate employee relationship, whether or not there is apparent consent from the individual.

"Pastoral relationship" means:

a relationship between a cleric, employee, or volunteer and any person to whom such cleric, employee, or volunteer provides counseling, pastoral care, spiritual direction, or spiritual guidance or from whom such cleric, employee, or volunteer has received a confession or confidential or privileged information.

This leads us back to prayer. I once had a conversation with a college chaplain who told me that he was obsessed with a woman student who had sought his advice. When I asked him directly if his obsession had sexual overtones, he said it did. Then when I asked him, seemingly to him as a non sequitur, how his daily prayer life was going, he said that it was nonexistent and had been so for quite a while. After I raised this issue with him, this good man was quickly able to connect the dots between his impoverished prayer life and the way that this hazardous sexual attraction had taken him unawares. By maintaining our prayer lives we are better able to keep the focus of our ministerial conversations where they should always be — on God.

Self-honesty is also critically important in dealing with boundary hazards. The extent to which we are able to recognize unwanted and unhelpful attractions, and then to pray about them and to seek guidance from a trusted confidant about them, is the extent to which we will be able to contain them so that no one is harmed by them. Do I find myself always sitting next to the same person in a meeting or gathering? Is my banter with this person a bit more personal and suggestive than it should be? Am I thinking about a particular person frequently and seeking ways to get together when others who might need more of my attention are neglected? Am I uncomfortable in the presence of a particular person, or does that person seem to be uncomfortable with me? These are the kinds of penetrating questions to ourselves that can help us notice sexual attractions that might lead to harmful behaviors and that can be effectively addressed in prayer, conversations with a trusted colleague or supervisor, or in counseling.

## Self-Care

Just as any discussion of boundary hazards leads inevitably to questions about the quality of one's prayer life, so do they lead to the topic of how we as fellow pilgrims take care of ourselves not only spiritually, but emotionally and physically. Ministry and the spiritual pilgrimage are demanding undertakings. They can sap our reserves of emotional energy and make us less resilient to the stresses of the journey than we need to be when things get out of balance. It is often said that many if not most clergy are introverted. It is a mark of introverted persons that, while able to be in groups and to interact effectively with others, these interactions use up energy (as opposed to the extroverted person, who is actually energized by being with other people). But ministry and the sharing of a spiritual journey is by its nature an extroverted enterprise! So it is critically important that the chaplain find ways to become reenergized well before the point of running out of steam completely.

Shortly after I was ordained and assumed the role of college chaplain I ran into a fellow priest one Monday morning coming out of a bookshop in Princeton. I was wearing my clerical collar, but he was not. We began a friendly chat during which he mentioned that Monday was his day off and that he intended to treat himself to a long walk in the woods followed by lunch with his wife at their favorite restaurant. When I replied that Monday was also my day off, he pointedly asked, "Then why are you wearing your clerical collar?" As I stammered some lame excuse about some business that I just *had* to do that day he replied, "Well, my friend, that doesn't sound like much of a day off to me. I hope you'll be careful about that!" I rushed home, changed my clothes, and took my family to a park for a picnic. And I've never forgotten Jack's admonition. Indeed, Mondays are a sacred time of sabbath for my family, and everyone in my ministerial orbit—students, faculty, staff, and even my bishop— know and respect that this time must be preserved for us.

Chaucer's *Canterbury Tales* and medieval accounts of pilgrimages to Santiago de Compostela in Spain and other holy places remind us pilgrims on long journeys to take periodic rests. Taking time to have dinner with our friends and families a few evenings a week, taking a regular day off, and having periodic holidays, vacations, and longer sabbatical leaves are all part of resting for the long journey. The demands of ministry and the shared spiritual journey being what they are, it is important for the chaplain to develop a self-awareness about when a rest is needed. In addition to the "scheduled stops" like days off and vacations, it is sometimes necessary to make an unscheduled stop, which is even harder to do than to observe regular sabbath times. One has to overcome the serpent voice that says an afternoon at the cinema or the spontaneous drive in the country on a weekday are wasted times. On the contrary, these unplanned brief holidays from the pressures of the journey can be lifesavers in the literal sense, and a healthy example to others.

Good habits of self-care are, to be sure, necessary to a long and productive ministry. They have another advantage that is often over-looked and is particularly critical in a university setting. Modern university students are driven by all the siren calls of the competi-tive commercial world. Every aspect of their environment tells them constantly that they must be achieving the next rung on the ladder of success. University students often joke about being a "slacker" if they take the time to so much as read a short work of fiction "just for fun." Their parents, their future employers, their classmates, and their teammates all are models of unrelenting striving toward an elu-sive goal of "success." The lives of top university students are thus devoid of balance. These lives know nothing of rest, silence, relaxed conversation, the quiet enjoyment of the company of another person. How necessary it is, then, for the chaplain as fellow pilgrim to model an alternative approach to life — a life that balances goal-directed work with prayer, relaxation, and the recharging of batteries. The chaplain's own habits of self-care can thus be a powerful aspect of his or her ministry and a great gift to all those driven students, faculty, and staff with whom the chaplain interacts.

## Sharing the Journey

The Christian pilgrimage is made in the company of others, and in this chapter we have been considering the ways in which the chaplain as pilgrim is a leader for university students who are typically less experienced and knowledgeable in their journeys toward God and whose lives have typically not achieved the kind of balance that is the sign of spiritual health. But there is an aspect of mutuality in the Christian pilgrimage that is equally important. As with any journey, there are times when everyone takes a turn as a leader and as a follower and when even the designated leader is helped along by those who have just recently joined the journey. Being mindful of this simple reality reminds us of our task to equip students to be leaders themselves.

Allowing others to lead us requires that we come to grips with the feelings of vulnerability that being led entails. Those of us who feel most comfortable when we are in charge will have a difficult time allowing others to share the role of leader. The need to appear to be in control of one's own journey and not to be in need of any assistance can not only be detrimental to one's own spiritual life, it can be an unhelpful model of spiritual self-reliance.

My own approach to life in general has always been one of self-reliance. I brought this trait with me to my ministry, and for a while it served me and those to whom I ministered quite well. I was always strong for others when they needed to be weak, and I was always available when someone needed help. But then I had my own life crisis. My only daughter — who was herself just finishing university — became ill with an incurable lung disease. In less than two years from the time she was diagnosed, she began to decline and eventually she died. I was devastated, of course, and I found that I could scarcely function for several weeks following her death. I was in no position to be of any assistance to anyone else. Fortunately, I was able to recognize this, partly as a result of the enormity of my daughter's death and partly as a result of loving advice from family and friends. Then I began to notice that several students with whom I had had many wonderful conversations about their own spiritual journeys were ministering to me. By visits, e-mails, or invitations to lunch each one showed a great deal of caring in a way that made it clear that nothing was expected of me. Each of these students put aside their own needs for spiritual guidance and gave me of themselves in a way that was truly full of God's grace. One young man — who later went to seminary — told me gently but quite bluntly and directly that no one expected me to function at my usual level during my time of acute mourning. This made it easier for me to pull back and take care of myself. Another young woman gave me a tape she had made of some of her favorite music that caused a great release of pent-up grief when I first listened to it.

This was a dramatic lesson in how God's grace often comes to us through other people. It was also a lesson in the mutuality of the Christian pilgrimage. Henri Nouwen wrote, " ... nothing can be written about ministry without a deeper understanding of the ways in which the minister can make his own wounds available as a source of healing."[46]

I remember being amused as a boy beginning to study Latin when my teacher — the one who kept just one chapter ahead of the class in the textbook — introduced us to the Latin word for baggage: *impedimenta*. All baggage, all the things we take with us on our spiritual journey, and all the obligations we have to ourselves and to others, whether big or small, must be balanced or else they will indeed be impediments. The ancient pilgrims to Jerusalem, or Canterbury, or Santiago de Compostela carried their baggage on their backs or loaded it on pack animals. When the loads were balanced, good progress was made; when they were lopsided and out of balance, the going was slow and frustrating. The challenge for the chaplain as pilgrim is to keep the big things and the little things in balance and by doing so help others to do the same.

My friend Jeanne Person, a Princeton alumna and an Episcopal priest whose vocation was sparked by her involvement with Princeton's campus ministry, sagely observes, "The change you experience each year is grace. Christianity is a movement, not an institution!"[47]

And so the journey continues.

Chapter 9

# Notes on the Ecumenical and Interfaith Challenge

——— ✠ ———

I HAVE TRIED to present a practical guide to campus ministry from the perspective of a chaplain working within a particular Christian denominational context, since this is the daily reality for me and many university chaplains. Equally, though, this daily reality is marked by a religiously diverse environment in which college students, faculty, and staff live and work alongside others of different religious traditions.

And therein lies the challenge: namely, how we shall make the most of this religious diversity while being faithful to our own traditions. And how might we embrace the practical opportunities to make resources go further by forming partnerships across denominational boundaries?

There is no such thing as "religion" apart from faith, and faith exists in some particularity, differing for each person and for each tradition. That particularity is a pearl of great price — for mutual growth and enrichment. It is also the basis upon which real progress can be made, if not in total organic unity among Christians, then at least in mutual respect and understanding that can lead to some forms of cooperation, shared worship and ministry, and common mission. Because such mutual respect and understanding can be the basis for a more peaceful world, as my friends on the mathematics faculty are fond of saying, this is a "nontrivial" matter.

When we think of this challenge, we tend to think according to what we can and cannot do in ecclesiastical terms. For example, Anglicans, Protestants, Orthodox, and Roman Catholics cannot share the Eucharistic table and share fully in the sacramental life of the church. There are also certain subjects that are taboo in mixed company, such as the possibility of the ordination of Roman Catholic women where that church is represented officially. These limitations of an ecclesiastical nature tend to limit our thinking and obscure the fact that there are many ways to worship God other than sacramentally (using a narrow definition) and that there is a whole world outside the church that needs us, and thus many ways for us to collaborate with one another.[48]

## So How Do We Do It?

Friendships and hospitality are the beginnings of ecumenical dialogue. I have already mentioned the meetings of campus ministers of all faiths that are regularly held at Princeton. Many campuses have such opportunities for interfaith dialog based on personal friendships. The friendships between campus ministers of different faiths model interfaith conversations for students, faculty, and staff. Although there are many old and tired jokes about the priest, the minister, and the rabbi having lunch, nothing models interfaith dialog so dramatically as the sight of several chaplains of different faiths enjoying one another's company and a meal in a public and visible place on campus. I regularly have coffee with my Roman Catholic counterpart at Princeton, and a strong friendship has developed between us. This friendship is not only a source of joy and of a great deal of mutual support for each of us, but also allows us to collaborate on sensitive pastoral issues when students or others are, for various reasons, living at the boundary of our two churches.

Friendships among chaplains can lead to many opportunities for service and worship that highlight our commonalities instead of our differences. Father Tom, the Roman Catholic chaplain just mentioned, has a long-standing friendship with the Lutheran chaplain that resulted in a joint Catholic-Lutheran prayer service every Tuesday night. Recently they have both invited our ministry to join them in offering this service, so now it's a threesome! A few years back a friendship between Princeton's Presbyterian and Jewish chaplains led to a joint trip to Israel. Other examples abound and point to the many benefits of chaplains seeking out colleagues on their campuses for informal meals, coffee breaks, and other social meetings that can lead to more meaningful relationships and joint efforts.

Formal opportunities for chaplains of all faiths to meet regularly are at times officially sanctioned by the university and hosted by whoever has overall responsibility for religious life on campus. At other institutions chaplains meet more informally on their own, often at the suggestion of one or two chaplains who take the initiative to organize a meeting. Chaplains at colleges that do not have such meetings may wish to find ways to get their colleagues together periodically, perhaps by hosting a luncheon or some other informal "getting acquainted" gathering.

From humble beginnings as social gatherings and progressing to opportunities for shared learning and mutual support, formal or informal associations of campus ministers from various faiths can lead to opportunities for joint worship services. For example, an interfaith opening convocation at the beginning of each academic year or a baccalaureate service at the time of commencement are opportunities for ecumenical worship that can involve people of all faiths. Special services at Christmas or during Holy Week, such as an ecumenical Maundy Thursday service, are other ways for Christians to worship together across denominational lines. For example, the rite of the washing of feet on Maundy Thursday is ecumenically accessible in ways that the Lord's Supper is not. And where there is full communion between denominations such as between the Episcopal Church in the U.S.A. and the Evangelical Lutheran Church of America or between the Methodist Church and the Presbyterian Church, even more can be done in the way of joint worship. A strong United Campus Ministries organization at Princeton led several years ago to the formation of a Student Interfaith Council, which is an organization of students of all faith traditions — Christian and non-Christian alike — who wish to learn more about and celebrate the richness of various religions traditions. Princeton's program has become a model for similar interfaith campus groups around the world.

Some campus ministries may find it desirable to link up with their counterparts from other denominations to form more formal organizations that pool resources and efforts. For example, at the Massachusetts Institute of Technology there is a joint Episcopal and Lutheran campus ministry. The two chaplains share all aspects of their ministry and alternate weekly between Episcopal and Lutheran forms of worship and sometimes worship according to liturgies they have jointly developed. Similarly, at the College of New Jersey a local Episcopal priest and a local Lutheran pastor have explored working together to develop a new joint ministry at that college.

Interfaith and interdenominational Christian worship as well as formal interdenominational campus ministry organizations highlight the chief benefits and the chief challenges of such collaborative efforts. Doing things together ameliorates the scandal of separation and fosters greater understanding and even affection among people of different faiths or traditions. Joint efforts can lead to better stewardship of money, buildings, and other resources by focusing on abundance rather than scarcity. But just as the benefits are many, so are the challenges.

Meaningful ecumenical work is time consuming. It requires that we spend the time and take the effort to listen carefully to one another. Imagine, for example, a Baptist, a Mennonite, and an Episcopalian planning a joint Maundy Thursday service. Further, imagine that the Episcopal chaplain suggests including the ceremony of the washing of feet, an annual event in most Episcopal and Roman Catholic congregations. The Baptist chaplain might never have participated in such a service and would need to have it explained. While the Baptist would readily grasp the biblical warrant for such a ceremony, it would also likely seem odd and slightly foreign, if not "over the top." The Mennonite chaplain, on the other hand, would likely react by saying, "Yes, we do that *often!*" Differences in liturgical styles and practices usually represent the tip of very large icebergs and call for a consider-able amount of sensitivity and mutual respect for different traditions and tastes. This requires serious and full discussions that unpack all the practical, theological, biblical, and, yes, emotional issues related to the service that is being planned. A failure to cover all these is-sues carefully and with great respect and sensitivity can lead to hurt feelings and can end up doing more harm than good.

As conversations about joint worship services progress, other is-sues will arise. One potentially sensitive issue is what to call the service in the first place. For example, a friend of mine recalls a Methodist chaplain telling him that her Roman Catholic counter-part would not participate in an ecumenical "worship" service since the word "worship" implied to him both word *and* sacrament. Being careful about this issue at the outset will avoid later difficulties.

Another sensitive issue is that of the need for everyone to give up something in order to gain the benefits of joint worship. For ex-ample, a joint Christian service that seeks to include all Christians on campus will not be a communion service since some Christians (e.g., Roman Catholics, Eastern Orthodox, some Lutherans, and others) are prohibited from taking communion in such services. As sad as it is for some to refrain from including communion in a joint service — since doing so actually *accentuates* the divisions among Christians — a greater sadness would result in a communion service that would in-clude some Christians and not others. Even where the issue of sharing communion — surely the most painful ecumenical issue among Chris-tians — is concerned, almost any ecumenical service requires some to do things that they would not normally do (e.g., washing of the feet on Maundy Thursday) or to forbear doing something they normally would do (e.g., chant a psalm instead of saying it). At other times, a matter of indifference to some that is important to others can usu-ally be negotiated amicably (e.g., including an invocation of the Holy Spirit in a communion prayer). This issue of giving something up often can seem trivial in the abstract. But when confronted with its reality in an actual situation, it can at best engender feelings of acute discomfort and at worst lead to a wish to abandon the ecumenical enterprise altogether.

And so we come to the need to speak truthfully about differences when they arise. Ecumenical relations have gotten a bad name largely because some folks obscure differences between Christian denominations or between various faith traditions. Obscuring real differences or pretending that they are not important will never lead to real and lasting ecumenical progress, but will lead only to misunderstandings and even suspicion. On the other hand, openness about theological differences can lead to greater respect and to finding ways in which people of various traditions can worship God in spite of differences. Indeed, those differences can even become the seasoning for the stew!

Sometimes the differences between various Christian groups and between Christians and non-Christians can loom so large that they are insurmountable obstacles. Though positive leadership by the chaplain can overcome many of these obstacles, sometimes it is best to hold off on certain types of partnerships and collaboration. Adam Kittrell lists these seven warning signs that joint ministries may not work:[49]

1. Incompatible theology or approach to mission.

2. Little or no openness to new ideas or ways of doing things.

3. Emphasis on the resources you bring, with little interest in your understanding of ministry or mission.

4. Lack of flexibility in the process or structure and insensitivity to polity differences.

5. Significant differences in operational style or expectations of leadership.

6. Reluctance to move beyond mission outreach to incorporate students into an active body of worship, fellowship, and service.

7. Serious resistance and no volunteers from within your congregation.

In addition to worship and formal organizational structures, there are many other practical dimensions to the interfaith and inter-denominational aspect of campus ministry. At a very basic level there is hospitality that one group might extend to others. Many Christian and Jewish campus ministries in the United States extended warm hospitality to Muslim student groups in the aftermath of the terror-ist attacks of September 11, 2001, when those students were fearful of vengeful physical and verbal attacks. The Christian and Jewish groups offered these students rooms for meetings and prayer, and by making them feel welcome offered a kind of spiritual and emotional balm to the entire campus.

Various formal and informal ecumenical groups on campuses can hold periodic programs in which prominent faculty and administra-tors are asked to speak to students on topics of mutual interest. The Office of Religious Life at Princeton sponsors a series called "What Matters to Me and Why," which has featured everyone from the university's first woman president (a molecular biologist) to popular professors and sports coaches who have been remarkably open with students about the spiritual dimensions of their life's work. A vari-ation on this theme found in several colleges and universities is the "Last Lecture Series." Respected professors are invited to deliver a lecture that they are asked to imagine would be the last lecture on their subject that they would ever give. The interfaith audiences thus have rich opportunities to look for common elements in the spiritual lives of others and for the ways that spiritual dimensions intersect with the secular dimensions of people's lives, an issue of particular interest to university students.

Bible study groups that cut across traditions and denominational lines also offer wonderful opportunities for students to be challenged and provoked in positive ways about their beliefs. Groups composed of Jews and Christians of various denominations can have an ex-perience probing Genesis or the Psalms that would be impossible in a more narrow and one-dimensional group. Similarly, interfaith groups that explore theological issues of common concern — such as prayer, vocation, or theodicy — from a variety of perspectives can be enormously productive for everyone.

Returning to the point made earlier that friendships are the basis for any ecumenical endeavor, many campus ministries join with those of other faiths or denominations for shared study breaks. These are usually held in a dormitory or a student center during the days immediately preceding examinations and, college students being what they are, always involve food — fresh-baked cookies, ice cream, pizza, and the like. A Christian campus ministry, for example, might invite the members of a Jewish or Muslim campus group to meet them for hot cocoa and cookies, or, better yet, might offer to prepare and host an evening meal for Muslim students during Ramadan or for Jewish students during one of their holy days. In addition to its other benefits, such invitations require that the hosts be sensitive to the dietary restrictions and other religious and cultural requirements of their intended guests.

Joint service and educational trips are other ways to foster ecumenical dialogue and understanding. A trip during a university recess to a place where students can perform some useful work — say, for example, in the wake of a flood or an earthquake or some other natural disaster — can form lasting and meaningful bonds across faith and denominational boundaries. In like manner, an educational tour to a place where two or more campus ministry groups can learn more about their common and separate histories can be enormously beneficial for all. A group of Christians, Muslims, and Jews making a pilgrimage to Jerusalem or Anglicans and Roman Catholics and Presbyterians visiting historical sites in Britain related to their traditions are just two examples.

## Denominational Defensiveness

A chaplain who fears that her flock will be harmed by interfaith contacts will be unlikely to promote them. If there is a feeling that students should not be exposed to views — theological, biblical, political, or the like — that are at odds with those of one's tradition, then there is unlikely to be much contact. It is understandable that a chaplain who is deeply committed to a particular religious tradition might be a bit wary of contaminating the minds and hearts of impressionable students with views that at the least could raise questions and in extreme cases lead to defections. The problem is, of course, that conveying such wariness can have an effect quite the opposite of what is intended, making the forbidden fruit seem inordinately attractive.

Since faith during the college years is a work in progress for many students who are exploring their own faiths and appropriating a faith tradition for themselves, it makes more sense to me for chaplains to encourage rather than discourage the exploration of various theological traditions and forms of worship. Such encouragement, far from driving young people away, can give them a stronger basis for holding on to their own, newly appropriated religious tradition than otherwise would ever have been possible. As one's differences with another tradition are opened up and celebrated, they can also be strengthened. In those cases where a defection actually does occur, it will thus occur in the context of fully explored and examined options for seeking and finding God.

Any interdenominational effort or interfaith effort is no substitute for the real thing — full organic unity under the one roof of God's household. And since so much of what passes for ecumenism is really each of us holding on to whatever particular doctrine, polity, or worship style we believe is distinctive and without which we cannot be who we are, we will all have to be very patient before we find ourselves under that single roof. In the meantime we must, with great anticipation, view all divisions as merely provisional. But I believe that we are called by God to be hopeful about that far-off day when we are united. And I believe that campus ministries that create opportunities for interdenominational and interfaith dialog and cooperation can give us a delicious foretaste of what surely is to come. Indeed, it may not be too bold to hope that as campus ministries equip the saints for leadership they will actually hasten the day when we are all united by offering now a glimpse of what wonderful things are possible in the future.

Appendix 1

# A Taizé Service

*Seventh Sunday after the Epiphany*
*February 23, 2003*

———— ✠ ————

Taizé is an interdenominational monastic community in southeastern France where thousands of people from all over the world, young and old, gather weekly to pray, to search, to sing, to find personal reconciliation, and just to enjoy the serenity of the place. The worship at Taizé, marked by depth and simplicity, has little talk and lots of singing; we are encouraged to let go of our rationality for a moment and venture into the world of the intuitive. The a cappella chants are easy to sing and repeated often, much in the manner of the Zen mantra, not only so that people can join in as they feel comfortable doing so, but also so that, gradually, the rhythms of the chants synchronize with our own rhythms. Feel free to sing in whichever language you wish. The long silences, uncomfortable for some at first, leave room for whatever is ruminating in our spirits — and when we can break through our discomfort with them, the silences become miraculously fruitful. In the Eucharist with which this service culminates, our spirits are invited to become one in the living Christ. That happens not because we make it happen but because we let it happen. So relax, enjoy the peace, be yourself, and let God do whatever God will with this time.

# A Taizé Service

"Our Darkness" (#14)

Silence

Collect for the Seventh Sunday after the Epiphany

"Kyrie" (#4; *Kyrie eleison* = Lord have mercy)

A reading: Isaiah 43:18–25 (The Lord redeems Israel)

Silence

"Bless the Lord, My Soul" (#9)

Silence

Gospel: Mark 2:1–12 (Jesus forgives and heals a paralyzed man)

Silence

Homily: The Chaplain

Silence

Prayers of the People. *As we share our prayers with one another, we are able to be the Church for one another. Please respond to each petition, either silently or aloud. After each petition, we will sing #20, "O Lord, Hear My Prayer."*

The Peace: *Greet quietly those near you with the peace of Christ.*

"Jubilate Deo" (#23; two-part round)

The Great Thanksgiving (Prayer V, the Scottish Episcopal Church)
*Please stand.*

The Lord's Prayer (traditional)

Communion. *Please remain standing if you wish to receive, and sit after receiving. All are welcome to receive the Sacrament.*

"Ubi Caritas" (#49)

Jesus Remember Me
Jesus remember me, when you come into your kingdom,
Jesus remember me, when you come into your kingdom.

✠

*Ordinarily, Communion is followed by a thanksgiving prayer and a blessing. But the Eucharist itself is both thanksgiving and blessing. Therefore, during the final song when all have received Communion, the Celebrant will depart. Please feel free at that point to leave silently whenever you are ready.*

Appendix 2

# The Installation of Student Leaders

—— ✠ ——

**Celebrant:** Brothers and Sisters in Christ Jesus, the Holy Scriptures make plain that we are all baptized by the one Spirit into one Body, and given differing gifts for a variety of ministries for the common good. Our purpose tonight is to commission the leaders of [name of ministry] in the Name of God to the various ministries to which they are called.

## The Presentation of the Conveners and Cabinet

**Conveners Emeritus:** We present to you [names of chairpersons] to be admitted to ministry of [name of office] in [name of ministry] and we present the Cabinet Elect, here assembled, to be admitted to their ministry in this Church.

## The Examination

**Celebrant asks the Leaders Emeritus:** Are these persons you are to present prepared by a commitment to Christ as Lord, by regular attendance at worship, and by the knowledge of their duties, to exercise their ministry to the honor of God, and the well-being of God's church?

**Leaders Emeritus:** I believe they are.

**Celebrant addresses the Leaders Elect:** You have been called to a ministry in the church of God at [name of college or university]. Will you, as long as you are engaged in this work, perform it prayerfully and with diligence?

Cabinet: I will.

Celebrant: Will you faithfully and reverently execute the duties of your ministry to the honor of God, and for the common good of the members of the whole church of God?

Cabinet: I will.

## The Commissioning

Celebrant (Antiphon): The Lord gives wisdom; from his mouth come knowledge and understanding; he stores up sound wisdom for the upright; he is a shield to those who walk in integrity.

Congregation (Response): I am your servant; grant me understanding

Leaders Elect: that I may know your decrees.

Celebrant: O Eternal God, the foundation of all wisdom and the source of all courage: Enlighten with your grace [names of leaders elect], and so rule their minds, and guide their counsels, that in all things they may seek your glory and promote the mission of your Church; through Jesus Christ our Lord.

Congregation (Response): Amen.

Celebrant: In the name of God and of this congregation, I commission you in your work among us and the [name of college or university] community.

Congregation (Response): Amen!

Appendix 3

# The Christian Spin on Ethics — The Shift from Self to Other

———— ✠ ————

*Exodus 20:1–17*

The ten commandments.

*Leviticus 19:1–17*

Ritual and moral holiness.

Duty to the poor (leave part of field unharvested for poor — don't strip it).

Do not steal or lie or defraud.

Do not hinder the handicapped.

Be just and fair.

Uses word "neighbor."

Do not hate in your heart or bear a grudge.

*Leviticus 25*

Sabbatical year — 7th year.

Year of Jubilee.

The people of Israel are the servants of God in verse 55.

Free slaves, forgive debts.

### Deuteronomy 5:1–33

Covenant.

Ten commandments.

You must follow this way of life so that it will go well with you and you may live long in the land that you are to possess (5:33) — the *telos*.

### Isaiah 52–55

Suffering servant — he was despised and rejected (53:3).

He has borne our sins (53:4).

Promise of assurance to Jerusalem.

Invitation to abundant life (chap. 55).

### Amos

Prophet as servant.

In Amos 3:15 we learn that people of Israel had winter and summer houses. This is something previously only kings could boast about. The people of Israel are living like kings. In Amos 6:4–6 we hear of lots of leisure time and activities. The downside was the widening gap between rich and poor.

Invective against Israel. They oppress and then have the gall to take the fruits of their oppression into the temple as an offering to Yahweh.

Best summary of whole book of Amos 5:24: "But let justice roll down like waters, and righteousness like an ever-flowing stream."

### Matthew 5:1–12

The Beatitudes.

Poor in spirit → kingdom of heaven.

Mourn → comforted.

Meek → inherit the earth.

Hunger & thirst for righteousness→ filled.

Merciful → receive mercy.

Pure in heart → see God.

Peacemakers → children of God.

Persecuted for righteousness → kingdom of heaven.

Persecuted falsely → reward great in heaven with prophets.

## Matthew 25:31–46

Judgment of Gentiles.

Hungry.

Thirsty.

Stranger.

Naked.

Sick.

Prisoner.

## Luke 10:29–37

Who is my neighbor?

The answer is the Parable of the Good Samaritan.

Man beaten and robbed.

Priest passed him by.

Levite passed him by.

Samaritan took care of him.

## Romans 12:1–13:10

New life in Christ → do not be conformed to this world.

Differing gifts → but one body in Christ.

Marks of true Christian.

Genuine love.

Hold fast to good.

Show honor.

Contribute to needs of saints.

Hospitality.

Compassion.

Live in harmony.

Never avenge yourself.

Feed enemies.

"For in doing this you will heap burning coals on their heads" (12:21).

Being subject to authorities (13:1–7).

All authority comes from God.

If you want to be at peace with authority, live a good life.

Love one another (13:8–10).

Love your neighbor as yourself.

By loving you fulfill the law.

## 1 Corinthians 1:18–21

Divisions in the Church.

Be united in same mind and purpose.

Do not allow divisions so as to empty the cross of its power.

Christ the power and wisdom of God.

Message of cross is foolish to those who are perishing.

To those who are saved the cross is the power of God.

## 2 Corinthians 12:1–10

Paul's visions and revelations.

Paul tormented by Satan → asks God three times for relief.

God responds: "My grace is sufficient for you, *for power is made perfect in weakness.*"

"I am content with insults, etc. . . . for Christ . . . for whenever I am weak, I am strong" (12:10).

# Notes

———— ✠ ————

1. Kenneth Underwood, ed., *The Church, the University and Social Policy: The Danforth Study on Campus Ministries* (Middletown, Conn.: Wesleyan University Press, 1969).

2. Barbara Brummett, *The Spiritual Campus: The Chaplain and the College Community* (New York: Pilgrim Press, 1990).

3. Cathy Caimano, *Many Signs and Wonders: A Travel Guide for You* (New York: Episcopal Church Center, 2000).

4. See, for one good example, *www.anglicansonline.org*, and also see especially *www.anglicansonline.org/usa/edu.html*.

5. The Evangelical Lutheran Church of America has on its campus ministry Web site an excellent article describing various forms of peer ministry. See *www.elca.org/campusministry/resources/aboutlcm/peerministry*. This resource is a prime example of the kind of infrastructure support to local ministries that a national church office can offer at very little cost.

6. Kenneth Mason, *George Herbert, Priest and Poet* (Oxford: SLG Press, 1980), 18.

7. See the Web site of the Taizé community in France for more on this form of worship at *www.taize.fr*. A songbook, *Songs & Prayers from Taizé*, is available from GIA Publications, Inc., Chicago.

8. The same could be said for the approved service books of the Presbyterian Church (USA), the United Methodist Church, the Evangelical Lutheran Church of America, and others.

9. For a superb brief essay on this subject, see Ellen Charry, "Consider Christian Worship," *Theology Today* 58, no. 3 (October 2001): 281–87.

10. I am aware that the term "orthodoxy" is, in these tumultuous times, radioactive and possibly loaded with meanings I do not intend. By it I mean adherence to the Christian faith as traditionally understood by Anglicanism: One God, Two Testaments, Three Creeds (Apostles, Nicene, and Athanasian creeds), Four Councils (the councils of Nicea, Constantinople, Ephesus, and Chalcedon; some add the Second Council of Constantinople in 553, Third Council of Constantinople in 680, and Second Council of Nicea in 787), and Five Centuries (the doctrines, sacraments, and orders of ministry found in

the first five centuries of the church). For an excellent brief discussion of this see "Orthodox: Does the Term Fit for Episcopalians?" by C. Christopher Epting in *The Living Church*, January 18, 2004, 12–13.

11. Henri J. M. Nouwen, *Creative Ministry* (New York: Doubleday, 1971), 91.

12. Aidan Kavanagh, *Elements of Rite* (Collegeville, Minn.: Liturgical Press, 1990), 99–100. This is a "must read" for every priest who takes good liturgy seriously.

13. *A Manual for Priests of the American Church* (Cambridge, Mass.: Society of Saint John the Evangelist, 1978), 205.

14. See Appendix 2 for a form for the installation of student leaders.

15. For forms of reconciliation that can be used as is or adapted, see the Episcopal *Book of Common Prayer* (1979), 447–52, or the Presbyterian *Book of Common Worship* (1993), 485–88 and 1023–24. For an excellent treatment of this subject, see Martin Smith, *Reconciliation: Preparing for Confession in the Episcopal Church* (Cambridge, Mass.: Cowley, 1986).

16. For an excellent introduction to the subject see the Church Teaching Series published by Cowley Publications, Cambridge, Mass., and John M. Wood, *The Formation of Christian Understanding: An Essay in Theological Hermeneutics* (Louisville: Westminster/John Knox Press, 1981).

17. Articles of Religion VI, *Book of Common Prayer* (1979), 868.

18. Catechism, *Book of Common Prayer* (1979), 855–56.

19. For excellent treatments of this subject that would be good additions to the chaplain's bookshelf as well as resources for study groups, see Christopher Bryan, *And God Spoke: The Authority of the Bible for the Church Today* (Cambridge, Mass.: Cowley, 2003), and Michael Joseph Brown, *What They Don't Tell You: A Survivor's Guide to Biblical Studies* (Louisville: Westminster John Knox Press, 2000).

20. A good source for beginning a study of Anglican moral theology is Stephen Holmgren, *Ethics after Easter* (Cambridge, Mass.: Cowley, 2000).

21. The list comes from the Alpha Web page which contains additional information: *alphacourse.org/welcome/index.htm.*

22. From *www.everyvoice.net/viamedia/index.html,* the Via Media Web site.

23. Two excellent resources for a Pre-Theo group are Suzanne G. Farnham et al., *Listening Hearts: Discerning Call in Community* (Harrisburg, Pa.: Morehouse Publishing, 1991), and Parker J. Palmer, *Let Your Life Speak: Listening for the Voice of Vocation* (San Francisco: Jossey-Bass, 1999). Suzanne Farnham has also edited a study guide to accompany *Listening Hearts: Manual for Discussion Leaders* (Harrisburg, Pa.: Morehouse, 1995).

24. Some of the material in this chart is based on chapter 9 of William Sloane Coffin's *Passion for the Possible* (Louisville: Westminster John Knox Press, 2004).

25. *New York Times*, April 22, 2004, B5; *Sydney Morning Herald*, April 24, 2004.

26. Melvin I. Urofsky, *A Voice That Spoke for Justice: The Life and Times of Stephen S. Wise* (Albany: State University of New York Press, 1982), 91–92.

27. Private conversation with the author, May 4, 2004.

28. Psalm 78:29–30 (*Book of Common Prayer*, 1979).

29. Adam J. Kittrell, *The ABCs of Ministry to the Campus* (Valley Forge, Pa.: American Baptist Churches in the U.S.A., 1994), 12.

30. Two good books on endowments are: Edward C. Schumacher and Timothy L. Seiler, *Building Your Endowment* (San Francisco: Jossey-Bass, 2002), and Lynda S. Moerschbaecher, Barbara G. Hammerman, and James C. Soft, *Building an Endowment: Right from the Start* (Chicago: Precept Press, 2003).

31. Much of this information is covered in more detail in the excellent workbook by Charles E. Gearing, Frederick Oborn III, and Pamela S. Wesley, *Funding Future Ministry* (New York: Episcopal Church Foundation, 2000). A CD based on this manual is also available that has a complete set of financial policies which can be edited on a word processor and adapted for local use.

32. For information about how to register as a charity in the United Kingdom, see *www.charity-commission.gov.uk*. In the United States an organization will need to apply for 501(c)3 status from the Internal Revenue Service at the federal level and also for tax-exempt status at the state level, where laws vary.

33. Material used with the kind permission of Holliman Associates from their Web site, *www.hollimanassociates.com*.

34. *Cambridge Advanced Learner's Dictionary.*

35. Peter J. Gomes, *Sermons: Biblical Wisdom for Daily Living* (New York: Avon, 1998), xvi.

36. See, for example, ibid. Gomes's sermons are biblical — indeed, they are very faithful to the lectionary and the liturgical year — and they are very topical and relevant for a university audience.

37. I am pleased to report that the tense relations between our chaplaincy and the evangelical groups are a thing of the past. It is worth noting that the event that caused the rapprochement was a meeting of all campus ministries on the evening of September 11, 2001, to plan a joint vigil service. Once again, God has fetched some good out of tragedy.

38. Available at *www.episcopalparishservices.org/default.asp*.

39. *www.lsoft.com.*

40. Wilbert R. Shenk, "Missionary Encounter with Culture," *International Bulletin of Missionary Research* 15 (1991): 104–9.

41. I wish to acknowledge Culpepper's excellent commentary on Luke for suggesting this approach to understanding the missionary commissioning of the seventy in Luke 10. See R. Alan Culpepper, "The Gospel of Luke: Introduction, Commentary, and Reflections," in *The New Interpreter's Bible* (Nashville: Abingdon, 1995).

42. David J. Bosch, *Believing in the Future: Toward a Missiology of Western Culture* (Harrisburg, Pa.: Trinity Press International, 1995).

43. While a retreat from *curae* might have been the impetus for the rise of Western monasticism, retreating was always more of an ideal than a reality. Any monastic will tell you that life in a convent or monastery has its own peculiar forms of *curae,* and some we bring with us *wherever* we go.

44. There are, of course, many excellent books that will help people in their spiritual journeys. Among the best are almost anything by Henri J. M. Nouwen, Thomas Merton, Suzanne Guthrie, Margaret Guenther, and Kathleen Norris. Among the best classic works on the spiritual life are *The Cloud of Unknowing*, the writings of Julian of Norwich, *The Practice of the Presence of God* by Brother Lawrence, *The Spiritual Exercises* of Saint Ignatius Loyola, and Saint Benedict's *Holy Rule.*

45. Margaret Guenther, *Holy Listening: The Art of Spiritual Direction* (Cambridge, Mass.: Cowley, 1992).

46. Henri J. M. Nouwen, *The Wounded Healer: Ministry in Contemporary Society* (New York: Doubleday, 1972), xvi.

47. K. Jeanne Person, personal communication to the author, October 6, 2004.

48. I am grateful to Bishop John Flack, director of the Anglican Centre in Rome, for his valuable insights on this topic.

49. A. J. Kittrell, *The ABCs of Campus Ministry: A Practical Guide for the Congregation in Mission* (Valley Forge, Pa.: American Baptist Churches in the U.S.A., 1994), 30.

# The Chaplain's Bookshelf

—— ✠ ——

\* = Especially recommended

## Introduction: The Office of Chaplain

Brummett, Barbara. *The Spiritual Campus: The Chaplain and the College Community.* New York: Pilgrim Press, 1990.

Galligan-Stierle, Michael, ed. *The Gospel on Campus: A Handbook of Campus Ministry Programs and Resources.* 2nd ed. Washington, D.C.: United States Catholic Conference, 1996.

Gribbon, R. T. *Students, Churches, and Higher Education: Congregational Ministry in a Learning Society.* 2nd ed. Charlotte, N.C.: United Ministries in Higher Education, 1996.

Hammond, Mary Tuomi. *The Church and the Dechurched: Mending a Damaged Faith.* St. Louis: Chalice Press, 2001.

Kittrell, Adam J. *The ABCs of Campus Ministry: A Practical Guide for the Congregation in Mission.* Charlotte, N.C.: United Ministries in Higher Education, 1994.

\*Portero, Sam, and Gary Peluso. *Inquiring and Discerning Hearts: Vocation and Ministry with Young Adults on Campus.* Atlanta: Scholars Press, 1993.

Underwood, Kenneth, ed. *The Church, the University and Social Policy: The Danforth Study on Campus Ministries.* Middletown, Conn.: Wesleyan University Press, 1969.

## Chapter 1: The Chaplain as Pastor

Bohmer, Carol, and Andrea Parrot. *Sexual Assault on Campus: The Problem and the Solution.* Lanham, Md.: Lexington Books, 1993.

\*Caimano, Cathy. *Many Signs and Wonders: A Travel Guide for You.* New York: Episcopal Church Center, 2000.

Chandler, Russell. *Feeding the Flock: Restaurants and Churches You'd Stand in Line For.* Washington, D.C.: Alban Institute, 1998.

\*Dittes, James E. *Pastoral Counseling: The Basics.* Louisville: Westminster John Knox Press, 1999.

Hunt, Michael J. *College Catholics: A New Counter-Culture.* New York: Paulist Press, 1993.

*Kadison, Richard D., and Theresa Foy DiGeronimo. *College of the Over-whelmed: The Campus Mental Health Crisis and What to Do About It.* San Francisco: Jossey-Bass, 2004.

Kollas, Beth Boyer. *Campus Ministry in a World Living with HIV/AIDS.* Charlotte, N.C.: United Ministries in Higher Education, 1996.

Parks, Sharon Daloz. *Big Questions, Worthy Dreams: Mentoring Young Adults in Their Search for Meaning, Purpose, and Faith.* San Francisco: Jossey-Bass, 2000.

Perry, William G. *Form of Intellectual and Ethical Development in the College Years.* San Francisco: Jossey-Bass, 1999.

## Chapter 2: The Chaplain as Priest

Countryman, L. William. *Living on the Border of the Holy: Renewing the Priesthood of All.* Harrisburg, Pa.: Morehouse, 1999.

Job, Rueben R., and Norman Shawchuck. *A Guide to Prayer for All God's People.* Nashville: Upper Room Books, 1990.

*Kavanagh, Aidan. *Elements of Rite: A Handbook of Liturgical Style.* Collegeville, Minn.: Liturgical Press, 1990.

*A Manual for Priests of the American Church.* Cambridge, Mass.: Society of Saint John the Evangelist, 1978.

Nouwen, Henri J. M. *Creative Ministry.* New York: Doubleday, 1971.

*Smith, Martin. *Reconciliation: Preparing for Confession in the Episcopal Church.* Cambridge, Mass.: Cowley, 1986.

*Songs & Prayers from Taizé.* Chicago: GIA Publications, 1991.

Tutu, Desmond. *An African Prayer Book.* New York: Walker, 1995.

## Chapter 3: The Chaplain as Rabbi

Adams, James R. *So You Think You're Not Religious? A Thinking Person's Guide to the Church.* Cambridge, Mass.: Cowley, 1989.

*Brown, Michael Joseph. *What They Don't Tell You: A Survivor's Guide to Biblical Studies.* Louisville: Westminster John Knox Press, 2000.

*Bryan, Christopher. *And God Spoke: The Authority of the Bible for the Church Today.* Cambridge, Mass.: Cowley, 2003.

Episcopal Diocese of New York. "Let the Reader Understand: A Statement of Interpretive Principles by Which We Understand the Holy Scriptures." New York: The Diocese of New York and the Episcopal Church, 2002.

*Farnham, Suzanne G., et al. *Listening Hearts: Discerning Call in Community.* Harrisburg, Pa.: Morehouse Publishing, 1991.

Grenz, Linda L., ed. *In Dialogue with Scripture: An Episcopal Guide to Studying the Bible.* New York: Episcopal Church Center, 1997.

Gribbon, Robert T. *Developing Faith in Young Adults.* Washington, D.C.: Alban Institute, 1990.

Gumbel, Nicky. *Questions of Life: A Practical Introduction to the Christian Faith.* Colorado Springs, Colo.: Cook, 1993.

Holmgren, Stephen. *Ethics after Easter.* Cambridge, Mass.: Cowley, 2000.

Palmer, Parker J. *Let Your Life Speak: Listening for the Voice of Vocation.* San Francisco: Jossey-Bass, 1999.

Wood, John M. *The Formation of Christian Understanding: An Essay in Theological Hermeneutics.* Louisville: Westminster/John Knox, 1981.

## Chapter 4: The Chaplain as Prophet

Barndt, Joseph R. *Dismantling Racism: The Continuing Challenge to White America.* Minneapolis: Augsburg Fortress, 1991.

*Brueggemann, Walter. *The Prophetic Imagination.* 2nd ed. Minneapolis: Fortress, 2001.

Coffin, William Sloane. *Passion for the Possible.* Louisville: Westminster John Knox Press, 2004.

*Hauerwas, Stanley, and William H. Willimon. *Resident Aliens: A Provocative Assessment of Culture and Ministry for People Who Know Something Is Wrong.* Nashville: Abingdon, 1989.

Urofsky, Melvin I. *A Voice That Spoke for Justice: The Life and Times of Stephen S. Wise.* Albany: State University of New York Press, 1982.

## Chapter 5: The Chaplain as Steward

*Gearing, Charles E., Frederick Osborn III, and Pamela S. Wesley. *Funding Future Ministry: A Comprehensive Guide for Church Leaders to Encourage Planned Gifts in Support of Christian Ministries.* New York: Episcopal Church Foundation, 2000.

Hitchcock, Stephen. *Open Immediately: Straight Talk on Direct Mail Fundraising: What Works, What Doesn't, and Why.* Medfield, Mass.: Emerson & Church, 2004.

Lansdowne, David. *The Relentlessly Practical Guide to Raising Serious Money: Proven Strategies for Nonprofit Organizations.* Medfield, Mass.: Emerson & Church, 2004.

Moerschbaecher, Lynda S., Barbara G. Hammerman, and James C. Soft. *Building an Endowment: Right from the Start.* Chicago: Precept Press, 2003.

Robinson, Andy. *Big Gifts for Small Groups.* Medfield, Mass.: Emerson & Church, 2004.

Schumacher, Edward C., and Timothy L. Seiler. *Building Your Endowment.* San Francisco: Jossey-Bass, 2002.

### Chapter 6: The Chaplain as Herald

Brown, Robert McAfee. *Reclaiming the Bible.* Louisville: Westminster John Knox Press, 1994.

Farris, Stephen. *Preaching That Matters: The Bible and Our Lives.* Louisville: Westminster John Knox Press, 1998.

Gomes, Peter J. *Sermons: Biblical Wisdom for Daily Living.* New York: Avon, 1998.

Honeycutt, Frank G. *Preaching to Skeptics and Seekers.* Nashville: Abingdon, 2001.

*Long, Thomas G. *Testimony: Talking Ourselves into Being Christian.* San Francisco: Jossey-Bass, 2004.

### Chapter 7: The Chaplain as Missionary

*Bosch, David J. *Believing in the Future: Toward a Missiology of Western Culture.* Harrisburg, Pa.: Trinity Press International, 1995.

*Bowen, John P. *Evangelism for "Normal" People: Good News for Those Looking for a Fresh Approach.* Minneapolis: Augsburg Fortress, 2002.

Hanchey, Howard. *Church Growth and the Power of Evangelism: Ideas That Work.* Cambridge, Mass.: Cowley, 1990.

Hunter, George G. *The Celtic Way of Evangelism: How Christianity Can Reach the West...Again.* Nashville: Abingdon, 2000.

### Chapter 8: The Chaplain as Pilgrim

*Allen, Diogenes. *Spiritual Theology.* Cambridge, Mass.: Cowley, 1997.

*Guenther, Margaret. *Holy Listening: The Art of Spiritual Direction.* Cambridge, Mass.: Cowley, 1992.

*Herbert, George. *The Country Parson.* New York: Paulist Press, 1981.

Hughes, Gerard W. *God of Surprises.* 2nd ed. London: Darton, Longman and Todd, 1996.

Kelly, Jack, and Marcia Kelly. *Sanctuaries.* New York: Bell Tower, 1996.

Mitton, Karen, and Norman Suggs. *Fellowship Friends: A Guide for Mentoring New Members.* Nashville: Cokesbury, 1997.

Monks of New Skete. *In The Spirit of Happiness: A Book of Spiritual Wisdom.* Boston: Back Bay Books, 2001.

Nouwen, Henri J. M. *The Wounded Healer.* New York: Doubleday, 1972.

*Winner, Lauren F. *Girl Meets God: On the Path to a Spiritual Life.* Chapel Hill, N.C.: Algonquin, 2002.

## Chapter 9: Notes on the Ecumenical and Interfaith Challenge

Ariarajah, S. Wesley. *The Bible and People of Other Faiths*. Geneva: World Council of Churches, 1985.

Ben-Chorin, Schalom. *Brother Jesus: The Nazarene through Jewish Eyes*. Athens: University of Georgia Press, 2001.

*Braaten, Carl E., and Robert W. Jenson. *The Ecumenical Future*. Grand Rapids: Wm. B. Eerdmans, 2004.

―――. *In One Body Through the Cross: The Princeton Proposal for Christian Unity*. Grand Rapids: Wm. B. Eerdmans, 2003.

Forward, Martin. *Inter-Religious Dialogue: A Short Introduction*. Oxford: Oneworld, 2001.

Lazowski, Philip, ed. *Understanding Your Neighbor's Faith: What Christians and Jews Should Know About Each Other*. Jersey City, N.J.: Ktav Publishing House, 2003.

*March, W. Eugene. *The Wide, Wide Circle of Divine Love: A Biblical Case for Religious Diversity*. Louisville: Westminster John Knox Press, 2005.

McLaren, Brian D. *A New Kind of Christian: A Tale of Two Friends on a Spiritual Journey*. San Francisco: Jossey-Bass, 2002.

Raushenbush, Paul B. *Teen Spirit: One World, Many Paths*. Deerfield Beach, Fla.: HCI Teens, 2004.

Rudolph, Susanne Hoeber, and James Piscatori. *Transnational Religion: Fading States*. Boulder, Colo.: Westview Press, 1997.

Wheatly, Margaret J. *Turning to One Another: Simple Conversations to Restore Hope to the Future*. San Francisco: Berrett-Loehler Publishers, 2002.